Accountable Discipleship

Handbook for Covenant Discipleship Groups In the Congregation

David Lowes Watson

Understanding the early Methodist class meetings
and using their principles in small covenant
groups for supporting our discipleship today.

DISCIPLESHIP RESOURCES

MATERIALS FOR GROWTH IN CHRISTIAN FAITH AND LIFE

P.O. Box 189 • Nashville, TN 37202 • Phone (615) 340-7285

Revised 1986.

Unless otherwise indicated, all scriptural quotations are taken from the Revised Standard Version of the Holy Bible.

Library of Congress Card Catalog Number: 84-70057

ISBN: 0-88177-009-4

Contents

PART TWO: COVENANT DISCIPLESHIP GROUPS

CHAPTER SIX: The Formation of Covenant Discipleship Groups

CHAPTER SEVEN: The Group Meeting

CHAPTER EIGHT: Group Leadership

CHAPTER NINE: Opening Covenant Discipleship Groups
    to the Whole Congregation

Preface

This short guide for Covenant Discipleship Groups follows an important Wesleyan precedent: the early Methodist class meeting. It follows another Wesleyan precedent in that the concept evolved in response to the expressed need of Christians who wanted to make a deeper commitment to their faith. A number of Covenant Groups have been meeting for the past eight years, seeking the grace of God according to the simple and time-honored practices of the church. To produce a manual for their use is merely to articulate what they have discovered in their weekly meetings, and to provide materials with which to teach others a way to an accountable discipleship.

So it was with the early Methodist class meeting, which came about more by accident than design, and which functioned with a minimum of formality and with few printed regulations. Indeed, the impression we get from Wesley is that his written directives for the classes were incidental to the commitment and practical witness of those who met week by week to "watch over one another in love." Since this handbook has been prepared specifically for the forming of Covenant Discipleship Groups in congregations of the church, it treats these early Methodist origins very broadly. For those who are interested in pursuing the theology and history of the class meeting in more detail, there is a companion volume, also published by Discipleship Resources: *The Early Methodist Class Meeting: Its Origins and Significance.* This includes a full set of appendices, reproducing the rules of the early Methodist movement and some records of the class meeting not readily accessible.

The model for Covenant Discipleship Groups first took shape in Holly Springs United Methodist Church, North Carolina, where I pastored while writing a doctoral dissertation at Duke University on the early class meeting. Since then, the groups have been introduced to a number of congregations in the South Central Jurisdiction of The United Methodist Church, and on the campus of Perkins School of Theology, Southern Methodist University. Most recently at Perkins, the groups have been adopted for a new course in spiritual formation required of all students in their first year of study. In each instance, the pragmatism and inclusiveness of the format have permitted those who take part in the groups to accept one another, irrespective of widely differing religious experiences, and to support one another in Christian discipleship.

Of the many whose Christian witness influences the following pages, two must be mentioned. Jim Beal, minister of First United Methodist Church in Conway, Arkansas, has been a constant advocate of the groups, guiding them to maturity in his own congregation, and fostering their introduction to many more. His encouragement and Christian collegiality leave me very much in his debt. Merrill Hartman, attorney and counselor in Dallas, Texas, exemplifies the ministry of the *laos*, and touches countless lives with his openness to God's grace. Our many conversations about the call to discipleship have greatly enriched my own walk with Christ.

As Wesley himself acknowledged two hundred years ago, the class meeting was not new in the church. Nor are Covenant Discipleship Groups. But they are a means of grace which perennially falls into neglect, and it has become my conviction that the time is ripe for their revival as a means of fulfilling the call to discipleship in our age.

Perkins School of Theology   September 1983
Dallas, Texas

Preface to the Revised Edition

In 1984, Covenant Discipleship Groups were adopted by the General Board of Discipleship as a program of The United Methodist Church, generating a wide use of this handbook and the need for a new edition. This has provided an opportunity to incorporate many suggestions and insights from C.D. Groups now meeting across the country.

A special word of thanks is due to the General Secretary of the General Board of Discipleship, Ezra Earl Jones, at whose initiative this dimension of the Methodist tradition is once again in the bloodstream of the church. His leadership in the area of Christian discipleship is a significant component of our present connectional system. I am grateful to my colleague, Ray Sells, for his guidance and support through the Center for Congregational Life at the G.B.O.D.; and to George E. Koehler, J. Lee Bonnet, and Mary Pugh at Discipleship Resources, who have been unfailingly helpful and cordial in the task of revision.

It is a pleasure to record that my friends in the faith, whose contributions I acknowledged two years ago, have moved to further areas of Christian service, where they continue to provide leadership for Covenant Discipleship Groups. Jim Beal is now Superintendent of the Batesville District in the North Arkansas Conference of the U.M.C.; and Merrill Hartman is now Judge of the 303rd Family District Court, Dallas, Texas.

General Board of Discipleship,   July 1985
Nashville, Tennessee

Introduction

The Challenge of Christian Witness

It has never been easy to be a Christian, and the late twentieth century is no exception. In company with Christians across the ages, those of us who try to be faithful followers of Jesus Christ find ourselves living in a constant tension. We hear the call of the carpenter from Nazareth, and we respond with repentance and joy to his offer of salvation. But as we live out this salvation, the call becomes increasingly and disconcertingly direct. The more we learn about the life and teachings of this man who celebrated at Jewish weddings, who ate Jewish food, who walked the roads of Palestine and who sweated Jewish sweat, the more we find that his call is an invitation to discipleship which leaves nothing in doubt yet everything open.

He stipulates only one condition, but it proves to be unconditional: a trusting obedience. "Follow me," he said to Simon and Andrew (Matt. 4:18-22). No trial period to see if they liked it. No discussion about potential benefits. No mention of the prospect of a fulfilled life and personhood. The reward of following this particular rabbi would be nothing more or less than the privilege of sharing in his work.

In due course it would be clear to his followers how rich was that reward; but this would not and could not be their motive for answering his call. The decision to follow Jesus of Nazareth meant taking an unqualified risk, a willingness to abandon everything which the world held to be important for the sake of those things which were of eternal importance. His parables and teachings made that clear time and again: the hidden treasure (Matt. 13:44), the man who built bigger barns (Luke 12:13-21), the prodigal son (Luke 15:11-32), and the harsh directive that following him with integrity would mean hating one's family and friends (Luke 14:26).

1

The purpose for joining Jesus had to be a sharing of his vision of a New Age for this planet, and the conviction that he was the one who would bring it to pass. His word for this vision was the *kingdom*, a time when the will of God would indeed be done on earth as in heaven (Matt. 6:10): A New Age, when God would truly be acknowledged as God by all people, from the least to the greatest (Jeremiah 31:34). A New Age, when the wolf would dwell with the lamb, the leopard would lie down with the kid, the lion would eat straw like the ox, and the earth would be full of the knowledge of God as the waters cover the sea (Isaiah 11:8ff). A New Age, of good news for the poor, release for captives, sight for the blind, liberty for the oppressed (Luke 4:18-19). A New Age, when there would be neither Jew nor Greek, neither slave nor free, neither male nor female (Galatians 3:28).

And *now* was the time to expect this. The prophetic vision of the future had become a present reality in the person of Jesus Christ. *Now* was the Year of Jubilee. *Now* was the New Age at hand (Luke 4:21).

The Cost of Discipleship

We know that this vision ultimately led to his execution, a horrible and agonizing execution, and we know that many of his followers across the centuries have given their lives in his service. Again the late twentieth century is no exception. There continue to be Christians throughout the world whose discipleship exacts a high price as they face the harsh reality of injustice and oppression. Their stories come to us with disturbing regularity: a Roman Catholic archbishop slain at the altar of his church in El Salvador, in the very act of celebrating the Mass; a Methodist bishop in Bolivia, imprisoned, interrogated, and exiled; Pentecostal Christians in Russia, refugees from the political order in their nation; church leaders in South Africa, wrestling with a legacy of racial oppression as they seek integrity in their Christian witness. And in the United States, behind the prophets of the Sixties, there were nameless thousands whose witness, often at the cost of imprisonment, physical abuse, and even their very lives, brought their nation to a new understanding of its heritage of liberty and justice for all.

For those of us in the United States who belong to what is commonly known as the mainline Protestant church, this presents a very real dilemma. We try to maintain a faithful witness in our life and work, but we are acutely aware that our Christian discipleship is altogether less costly, and far less dramatic. We live our lives in the subtle grip of technological affluence, even when our share of it is quite modest. The challenges we face are more likely to be those of single parenting, overeating, teenage drug abuse, video addiction, unemployment, and professional competition. We are so consumed with meeting the daily struggle to survive the pressures of this affluence that we seem to have no energy—physically, emotionally, intellectually, or spiritually—to become involved with the struggles of the martyrs in our own country, never mind anywhere else.

Nor does it help to have our problems repeatedly diagnosed by sociologists, psychologists, or pulpiteers. We know our dilemma only too well. Those of us who are overweight are rarely encouraged by reminders that every two seconds a human being somewhere in the world dies of starvation. Those of us who are parents of teenage sons and daughters are unlikely to be heartened by the reminder that nuclear war is a lethal possibility. Deep down we know that we should either join with those Christians who protest against the arms race, or with those who affirm it as the surest balance of international power. We know that to take no position at all is the height of irresponsibility, yet that is exactly what most of us find ourselves doing. Those of us facing broken marriages, with bitter disputes over property and child custody, are seldom in the mood to hear arguments on the one hand for the liberation of women from male-dominated relationships, or on the other hand for the family as a Christian institution to be maintained at all costs.

Not that such analyses and exhortations are irrelevant. On the contrary, they have proved to be the cutting edge of Christian discipleship in our time, reminding us that the gospel impacts human relationships and social structures at every level of our existence. The dilemma is that, for most of us, the problems are at once more mundane and more immediate. Faced with such daily pressures at home and at work, our response to the larger vision of discipleship for the most part tends to be one of exasperation. "What can *I* do about the problems of the world? . . . *How* can I do anything?"

The Anguish of Discipleship

These are not empty questions. Most of us ask them with sincerity, at times with anguish, and would very much like to have them answered. In spite of the numbing effect of communication technics, we have been moved by the photographs of starving children staring at us with empty eyes and enlarged stomachs. We have been sickened by the stark remnants of the holocausts in our time: the mass graves, the torture chambers, the concentration camps. We have seen the repeated news-reels of bombings in Northern Ireland and Lebanon, and it has chilled us that two nations with strong economic and cultural ties should have sacrificed a thousand young lives in a remote South Atlantic battle.

But this is not all. As we see the continued evidence in the world of human rebellion against God, we find ourselves to be part of it. The commandment of Jesus was clear: that we should love God and love our neighbor as ourselves. But we find ourselves wondering whether we will ever be able to obey this command. "They will know we are Christians by our love," runs the well-known refrain. Well, on a good day, perhaps; but on most days, it would be difficult. And, with a harsh irony, Sundays seem to test us most of all. The routine is all too familiar: short tempers, bathroom bad manners, spoiled breakfasts, and last-minute scrambles to get to church. Then we glance across the street to our neighborly pagan, who is leisurely sniffing the morning before relaxing with the Sunday paper and a second cup of coffee. We might be forgiven for a moment of real doubt. Surely *we* are the ones who are supposed to have the love and peace of God!

We are indeed searching for answers, searching for God's will in our lives, for some assurance that in the midst of the tension in which we live, we are following the carpenter from Nazareth. Our minority broth-ers and sisters in the church—Hispanic, Black, Native American, Asian—remind us that God's salvation is a new order of justice as well as love. Our sisters and brothers throughout the world send us the gospel message with renewed missionary zeal, gently but firmly rebuk-ing us for our churchly self-centeredness and our abuse of the gospel as a spiritual analgesic. We hear their word, and it cuts us to the quick. We badly need to know how we can play our part in congregations which are no longer local, but global, and that our witness in these places of worship and outreach has a degree of integrity.

The Power of Discipleship

First of all, we can take heart from the Scriptures that the tension is not new. As Paul makes clear in his letter to the church at Rome, it is a dilemma as old as human sin. For when we truly hear the Word of God inviting us to repentance and forgiveness, the extent of our predicament strikes us with a critical self-awareness:

> I do not understand my own actions. For I do not do what I want, but I do the very thing I hate. Now if I do what I do not want, I agree that the law is good. So then it is no longer I that do it, but sin which dwells within me. For I know that nothing good dwells within me, that is, in my flesh. I can will what is right, but I cannot do it. For I do not do the good I want, but the evil I do not want is what I do. . . . For I delight in the law of God, in my inmost self, but I see in my members another law at war with the law of my mind and making me captive to the law of sin which dwells in my members. Wretched man that I am! Who will deliver me from this body of death? (Rom. 7:15-19,22-24).

The dilemma is resolved, as we know, by Paul's triumphant declaration in the following chapter:

> There is therefore now no condemnation for those who are in Christ Jesus. For the law of the Spirit of life in Christ Jesus has set me free from the law of sin and death. For God has done what the law, weakened by the flesh, could not do: sending his own Son in the likeness of sinful flesh and for sin, he condemned sin in the flesh, in order that the just requirement of the law might be fulfilled in us, who walk not according to the flesh but according to the Spirit. . . . For all who are led by the Spirit of God are sons of God. For you did not receive the spirit of slavery to fall back into fear, but you have received the spirit of sonship. When we cry, "Abba! Father!" it is the Spirit himself bearing witness with our spirit that we are children of God, and if children, then heirs, heirs of God and fellow heirs with Christ. . . . (Rom. 8:1-4,14-17a).

Theologians refer to this great truth as the doctrine of justification by faith, and it has been the taproot of Protestantism ever since the Reformation. It is the declaration by God in Christ that, in spite of our sin, in spite of our imperfections, *our best is good enough for God.* We are accepted by God, just as we are, warts and all. We are no longer measured by what we know we ought to do, nor yet by what others do; still less by what others tell us we ought to do. We are free from all such burdens, because we know that we are reconciled as members of God's family. Whatever the level of our accomplishment—and significantly, whatever the level of our commitment also—we have the deep joy and peace of knowing that we are once again in tune with the things of eternity.

The words of the old hymn are profound, and we should sing them thoughtfully:

> 'Twas grace that taught my heart to fear,
> And grace my fears relieved;
> How precious did that grace appear,
> The hour I first believed.[1]

Just as the inviting power of grace awakens us to the reality of our separation from God, the reconciling power of grace restores us to God's love. We know this because the carpenter from Nazareth promised it. And his promise holds true, because God raised him from the dead.

The Task of Discipleship

This was not the extent of his promise, however, nor was it the full purpose of his call. He appeared to his first disciples, not only to assure them of his victory over sin and death, but also to commission them for a task which lay ahead. That commission comes to us with the same challenge and the same promise. He challenges us to become his disciples in preparing for God's salvation of the world, and he promises us the privilege of his friendship. Moreover, this is the offer of a true friendship—a sharing of *everything.* As Paul goes on to say in Romans, we are heirs with Christ provided we suffer with him, in order that we might be glorified with him. Christ's victory over sin is not yet here in its fullness, and those who accept his call to discipleship must be ready for a struggle with themselves and with the world:

I consider that the sufferings of this present time are not worth comparing with the glory that is to be revealed to us. For the creation waits with eager longing for the revealing of the sons of God; . . . . We know that the whole creation has been groaning in travail together until now; and not only the creation, but we ourselves, who have the first fruits of the Spirit, groan inwardly as we wait for adoption as sons, the redemption of our bodies. For in this hope we were saved. Now hope that is seen is not hope. For who hopes for what he sees? But if we hope for what we do not see, we wait for it with patience (Rom. 8:18-19,22-25).

The message is at once exhilarating and sobering. However joyfully we might be reconciled to God as sons and daughters, however liberating it is to be accepted by God, our imperfections notwithstanding, there is a larger context for our discipleship. God's plan of salvation has global, indeed cosmic dimensions. Just as we have been given new life through our reconciliation with God in Christ, so God intends new life for the whole of creation. Just as our own rebirth comes through the labor and suffering of Jesus Christ, so does that of the world. As disciples of Jesus Christ we are called to share in that labor and suffering.

We have found personal forgiveness and reconciliation in Christ, but the consequence of this is a discipleship which sends us back into the world where once again we are confronted with the realities of sin and suffering and evil, including our own. The difference is that this time the sin and suffering are not just personal, but global and systemic: the injustice of oppression, the torment of disease, the scandal of starvation and the cheapness of human life. The joy and the freedom of personal discipleship lead us inexorably to the challenge of global discipleship, and this is what brings us face to face with our dilemma. How can we be obedient to Jesus Christ in a world which remains rebellious against God, not least because we still find rebellious tendencies in ourselves?

Needless to say, it is possible to avoid the dilemma by effecting a spiritual withdrawal from the world and finding a safe place to enjoy our new relationship with God. There are many such refugees in our churches, people seeking Christian fellowship as a means of running away from the realities of faithful discipleship. They look at the world with a jaundiced eye, forgetting that this is the planet which, with all its sin and evil, Jesus came to save. They fail to remember that God will go out to look for the lost sheep rather than stay with the ninety and nine in the fold. They seem oblivious to the parable in which the feast is given for the returned prodigal, not the son who stayed at home. They appear to be unaware of Jesus' warning that the criterion for being welcomed into the kingdom is not right belief, but right action (Matt. 25:31-46). The weight of the gospel is all too clear: *that the world is God's sphere of salvation, and disciples of the Savior must join him where he is at work.*

The Hope of Discipleship

There are those, of course, who argue that a discipleship patterned too strictly on the life and teachings of Jesus is unrealistic. Paul is right, their argument goes. The world is indeed waiting for a rebirth. But it won't happen this side of eternity, and in the meantime the world remains as imperfect as ever it was. We must therefore learn to live with these imperfections, trusting God to forgive us for the compromises we have to make. After all, there isn't much that can be done about the evil and suffering we see around us. The best we can do is to follow Christ faithfully in our daily lives, and trust God to deal in due time with these larger problems.

Even a cursory reading of scripture indicates that this view of Christian discipleship falls far short of the New Testament vision of God's salvation. Paul's message is one of hope—hope for the world as one day it will be, hope for the New Age announced and inaugurated by Jesus Christ. And those of us called to follow this Savior must not only share his vision of the New Age, but share it *to the fullest.* That is why the call comes with a word of warning: Be ready to share in the sufferings of Christ if you accept the name of Christian. The call to discipleship means nothing less than an emulation of Jesus in all aspects of our lives. Mistakes there will be, and shortcomings. But there must be no compromise of *intent.* We must be ready to give all in his service, if need be to the laying down of our lives.

At this point, many of us become apprehensive. Is this what Paul is suggesting to us in Romans 8? Is discipleship such a radical alternative that we must live in an impossible tension? Do the realities of a faithful Christian witness cancel out the freedom of our new relationship with God by taking us back to the dilemma of Romans 7—knowing what we ought to be doing in the world, but finding ourselves unable to do it? Is the only way to faithful discipleship the way of the martyr, taking Christ's words literally, giving away all that we have in order to feed the poor, and following him to the cross? As we have noted, there are Christians in our day and age who make precisely that witness, showing us that it is indeed possible to sell everything we have for the poor, and to live simply in the midst of affluence. Should we not be doing likewise?

As with the dilemma of our call, the answer to this dilemma of our commission lies with God's grace. Christ does not ask more of us as his disciples in the world than we are able to accomplish in the love and power of the Holy Spirit. With the call to discipleship comes the promise of grace to sustain us in the journey which lies ahead.

> Through many dangers, toils and snares
> I have already come;
> 'Tis grace that brought me safe thus far,
> And grace will lead me home.[2]

On my kitchen wall is a plaque given to me many years ago by a woman who knew the truth of what it says: "The will of God will never lead you where the grace of God cannot keep you." God has not forgiven us our sins and weaknesses in order to lay fresh failures on us. Christ does not ask of us anything we are not able to carry out in the strength of his Spirit. "Thanks be to God," said Paul, "through Jesus Christ our Lord. . . . You are not in the flesh, you are in the Spirit, if in fact the Spirit of God dwells in you" (Rom. 7:25, 8:9).

The Condition of Discipleship

Yet in the very resolution of our dilemma there is an important proviso. Yes, God will sustain us in whatever we are called to do. And yes, nothing in the whole of creation, even a creation in the birthpangs of new life, can separate us from the love and the power of that grace— nothing, that is, save our freedom of choice. For the grace of God is so gracious that we are always given the choice of accepting it or rejecting it—and this is what ultimately makes our discipleship costly. Paul reminds us of it over and over again in Romans 8: *If* the Spirit of God is within us; *if* we join with Christ in his suffering; *if* we are children of God; *if* we hope for what we do not see; *if.* . . . Further on in the epistle, Paul makes the point even more forcefully:

I appeal to you, therefore, brethren, by the mercies of God, to present your bodies as a living sacrifice, holy and acceptable to God, which is your spiritual worship. Do not be conformed to this world but be transformed by the renewal of your mind, that you may prove what is the will of God, what is good and acceptable and perfect (Rom. 12:1-2).

Not an appeal, we should note, to exercise a self-discipline, or an exhortation to strive for global transformation, the advice is at once more simple and profound: let God's grace work in our lives. For the grace of God is the only strength in which we can be faithful disciples. The key word in all of this is *obedience*, and the fundamental question for the Christian, therefore, must always be, "How do I know that I am obedient? How do I know that what I am doing is the will of God?"
Paul's answer is once again to affirm the grace of God:

Likewise the Spirit helps us in our weakness; for we do not know how to pray as we ought, but the Spirit himself intercedes for us with sighs too deep for words. And he who searches the hearts of men knows what is the mind of the Spirit, because the Spirit intercedes for the saints according to the will of God. We know that in everything God works for good with those who love him, who are called according to his purpose (Rom. 8:26-28).

In other words, Christians who accept the grace of God, who permit the strength and the power and the love and the peace of God to work in their lives, have the assurance of an obedient discipleship. It will not be a perfect discipleship, but it will be the best that they can offer, and it will be wholly acceptable to God. Christians who endeavor to be disciples *without* this grace, however, will lack the capacity for obedience, and will find themselves still caught in the dilemma of knowing what ought to be done, but never able to do it. Such Christians never have peace of mind, are filled with constant uncertainty, and are persistently stung by the witness of those whose discipleship is more costly.
If we can accept the word of countless clergy and laity across the land, this is where a large number of American Christians find themselves today. They are constantly trying to do the best they can in the ambivalences of the world in which they live and work, but they are

never sure that their best is good enough for God. Contrary to the thoughtless and self-righteous critic who charges that the average American Christian has little more than a folk religion, there are many in our churches who are willing and ready to make a deeper commitment to their discipleship. The question is how to make that commitment reliably and faithfully. If there is a quality common to most American churchgoers, it is sound common sense, and we have rightly become suspicious of contemporary forms of spirituality which extol the development of human personhood to the neglect of God's work in the world. We are equally and astutely mistrustful of exhortations to a worldly involvement which seem to render the grace of God peripheral to the task in hand.

The Practice of Discipleship

Faithful discipleship lies rather in certain well-tried practices through which Christians across the centuries have opened themselves to God's grace. John Wesley referred to these disciplines as the *means of grace*, and instilled in the early Methodists the necessity of using them as often as possible. As with so many of Wesley's guidelines for discipleship, this instruction has the ring of sound common sense. If the call of Christ to discipleship does make requirements of us; and if these requirements can be met only by availing ourselves of God's grace—something which is clear to any Christian who has tried to meet them in his or her own strength alone; and if the church has found across the centuries that there are certain reliable channels for this grace; then good sense must surely dictate that Christians use these means of grace in the fullest possible way. By the same token, if Christians are not using these means of grace, and as a result are finding their discipleship fraught with ambivalence and uncertainty, then we should be asking ourselves with some urgency *why* we are not using them.

The early Methodists asked themselves this question, and their answer, as we might expect, was practical and down-to-earth. It came home to me many years ago when I was a student at Oxford University. Like most new students, I arrived with all sorts of good resolutions to make the best of my time and opportunities. Perhaps more than most, I was resolved to be "methodical," being very aware that this had been Wesley's place of study more than two hundred years earlier. One of my resolutions was that I was going to keep physically fit, and I decided that a good way to do this would be to go for a run each morning before breakfast. The first week, I ran every morning. Breakfast took on new meaning, and I felt invigorated and refreshed for the day's work. The second week, I missed a couple of mornings. The third week, I missed all but one morning. The fourth week I missed altogether, and the fifth week I made an amended resolution—that *next* year I would go running each morning!

The following year, however, I took a precautionary measure. I asked the person next door if he would like to go running with me. "Good idea," he said. And with somewhat mixed feelings, I knew I was committed. On the days I was late, he would bang on my door with a cheery word: "Time to be going!" There were several mornings, by no means as many, when I would return the favor. Occasionally, we would both be late, and would spring out of our rooms simultaneously, insisting that we were just about to come and get the other! We made it all through the year, every morning.

There is no need to explore this as a phenomenon of the human will. It merely illustrates that some things are done better by two people than by one. We find it in every walk of life. Meals tend to be better planned and cooked when there is more than one person at the table. Construction engineers on a building site find a workmate indispensable. Airline pilots doing a pre-flight check rely on each other's memory. Sanitary engineers collecting garbage need a team to drive and pick up at the same time. Mountaineers roped together for a climb, athletes pacing one another for a race, all need the help and support of others. In short, anything which is subject to human limitation or error requires the collegial presence of another person to ensure reliability. It is a fact of life.

Yet as Christians, we persistently neglect to apply this principle to the most basic requirement of our discipleship—making sure that we avail ourselves of the means of grace. Little wonder, then, that we find ourselves constantly searching for the meaning of our Christian commitment. By failing to help one another to be open to God's grace, we are deliberately opting for self-sufficiency in our discipleship; and that, as we have clearly seen in scripture, is a contradiction in terms. To use Wesley's vivid language, it means that we are making shipwreck of our faith.

Self-sufficiency is also the reason why the call of the Holy Spirit in our time to a new and deeper commitment to discipleship is often rejected as impracticable. It is clear that most people who worship on a Sunday morning have no intention of selling all that they have to feed the poor and clothe the naked. Still fewer take stands on issues of social justice. As a result, church-going and costly discipleship are perceived to be contradictory, and church becomes the place where people go chiefly to be helped, not challenged. H. Richard Niebuhr's famous *dictum* is turned inside out. Instead of the gospel comforting the afflicted and afflicting the comfortable, it pampers the comfortable to the neglect of the afflicted—and for no other reason than that the alternative seems to be impossibly unrealistic. What is needed is some practical format for the exercise of costly discipleship *within* the average American congregation.

A Pattern for Discipleship

There are United Methodists who believe that our heritage in Wesley's early Methodist societies provides us with just such a model: the *class meeting*. It was a weekly gathering, a sub-division of the society, at which members were required to give an account to one another of their discipleship, and thereby to sustain each other in their witness. These meetings were regarded by Wesley as the "sinews" of the Methodist movement, the means by which members "watched over one another in love."[3] They were grounded in solid theological principles which could readily be grasped, making them not only a point of mutual accountability, but also a rich traditioning of the gospel. The early Methodists helped one another to plumb the depths of the scriptures and the teachings of the church. They drank deeply from the well of the gospel at a time when there were many shallow ponds offering mere reflections of the Word.

In short, they practiced their discipleship with integrity—by availing themselves of the means of grace. It's high time we took the necessary steps to follow their example. Sin has very little to do with our present dilemma. It's a failure to exercise common sense.

For Thought and Discussion

1. What does it mean to you when you pray, "Thy kingdom come, thy will be done on earth as it is in heaven"?

2. Has your Christian witness proved costly? Rewarding?

3. How should Christians in an affluent culture respond to the witness of costly discipleship in the midst of poverty or oppression?

4. Has the dilemma expressed by Paul in Romans 7 been resolved in your life?

5. What do you think is meant by the statement on page 8, *"that the world is God's sphere of salvation, and disciples of the Savior must join him where he is at work."*

6. "Mistakes there will be, and shortcomings. But there must be no compromise of *intent*," (page 8). Discuss.

7. "The will of God will never lead you where the grace of God cannot keep you" (page 9). Has this been true in your Christian life?

8. Do you agree that the present dilemma of our discipleship is a failure to exercise common sense (page 13)?

Part One

Early Methodist
Discipleship

The early Methodists worked out their salvation in the reality of worldly living, empowered through the means of grace afforded by the time-honored disciplines of the church. They did this by exercising a mutual accountability for their discipleship in the context of Christian fellowship.

Chapter One

Wesley's Understanding of Christian Discipleship

The spiritual and churchly pilgrimage of John Wesley made him especially suited to lead the early Methodist societies into a practical understanding of what it meant to be a Christian in the world. He was empowered by the spirit of discipleship, and he applied it through structures from which we still have much to learn. His upbringing in the Church of England had instilled in him the importance of the Christian tradition, and especially of the church as a visible institution. At the same time, his encounter with Moravian pietism gave him a deep sense of personal salvation in Christ and the power of God's transforming grace in the life of the sinner.

Grace and Obedience in the Christian Life

The distinctive quality of early Methodist discipleship is that both of these emphases were evident in the life and work of the societies. On the one hand, there was the offer of salvation through Christ, in which the inviting grace of God brought the sinner to forgiveness and reconciliation—a new relationship with God, a new birth. Yet in order to maintain this new relationship, there had to be a life of obedient discipleship in which the grace of God could change the forgiven and reconciled sinner. Not only was this discipleship necessary to strengthen and develop the witness of the Christian. Without it, the new relationship with God was repudiated, and faith was rendered meaningless.

This emphasis on obedience provided the early Methodists with a deep sense of assurance. Regardless of how a person might experience this new relationship with God, one could do one's best to be an obedient disciple, and *know that this would be acceptable to God*. The

17

rules of the societies stated explicitly that the only condition for admission to membership was a *desire* to be a Christian, whether or not one could claim to have had a particular Christian experience. But to *continue* in a Methodist society, one had to give evidence of this desire by avoiding evil, doing good, and using the means of grace instituted by the church and proven in practice. Discipleship meant following the commandments of Christ according to the law of love, and could therefore be attempted by anyone who was willing to follow some very basic rules for daily living.

This is what makes the early Methodist class meeting such an important paradigm for Christian discipleship. Yes, it was a means by which the faith of a new relationship with God in Christ could be shared in open fellowship. But it was also a point at which Christians gave an account of what they had *done* in obedience to Christ, a place where they could receive guidance and, if need be, correction from one another. There was an accountability to be exercised as well as an experience to be shared, and these weekly meetings were the occasion of both. It was the genius of the Methodist movement in Wesley's day, and is perhaps the most important contribution Methodism can make to the contemporary world church.

Yet we cannot adopt this paradigm without an important qualification. The class meeting can help us with our contemporary discipleship only if it is *traditioned,* that is, understood in its own context and then appropriated for contemporary Christian witness in the world. This is all the more important because we happen to live in a culture where small groups have become recognized as useful and necessary components of our social fabric. Most especially in the church, they serve to strengthen and sustain the spontaneity of fellowship, best described by the scriptural word *koinonia.* There is no doubt that these groups accomplish much for persons neglected or discarded by a technological society, and they most certainly provide a useful service for those who look to the church for the community they cannot find elsewhere. But there was more, much more, to the early Methodist class meetings than mere fellowship.

These weekly gatherings were first and foremost designed to equip Christians to be authentically Christian in a world which was largely hostile to their message. The early Methodists believed that they had received a direct commission to go into the world, and to join the risen Christ in the task of proclaiming God's salvation in the power of the Holy

Spirit. The class meeting was where they came to share the bumps and bruises of this encounter, to comfort and strengthen one another, and to provide a *mutual accountability* for the task in hand. It is this we must keep in mind as we examine the class meeting as a model for discipleship today.

Wesley and the Christian Tradition

To do so, we must turn first of all to John Wesley and the tradition he himself appropriated and handed on. It is a task rendered at once easy and difficult by the nature of his ministry. On the one hand, his journal and his letters give us perhaps the most complete record of any church leader's life and work, helping us to know him as a human being with limitations as well as strengths. On the other hand, precisely because this detailed record is so fascinating, it is easy to overlook the theological foundations of his ministry. Moreover, he was an evangelist, and true evangelists are always in touch with the world—something which can prove disconcerting to those of us who live our lives within the safety of church walls. Albert Outler has put it well: Wesley was not "a theologian's theologian. His chief intellectual interest, and achievement, was in what one could call a folk theology: the Christian message in its fullness and integrity, in 'plain words for plain people.' " [4]

This concern to make theology relevant for common people and to take the Christian message to as many as possible prevented Wesley from leaving us with a detailed exposition of the Christian faith. Yet his writings, when read in the context of his ministry, articulate with remarkable clarity the essential tension of the Christian faith: the vision of the gospel and the reality of worldly living. Wesley came to understand this tension because he exercised his ministry among ordinary, humble Christians, as they tried to live out their faith in the world. Indeed, it is this which arguably makes him the most significant church leader in Protestantism. He took seriously the reaction of people to the message he and his preachers proclaimed, because he found that the faith of these simple people had as much integrity as the teachings of the church. At the same time, however, he granted full authority to the laws and doctrines of the Church of England, and was critical of those who would not affirm or practice what they prescribed.

The polity of the early Methodist societies was forged in this tension between Wesley as a church theologian, concerned for the Christian tradition, and Wesley as practical churchman in the field, concerned for the spread of the gospel and for the building up in the faith of those who responded to the message he proclaimed. Time and again, what at first sight appears to be mere pragmatism proves to have been based on sound theological principles and a weighty concept of the church.

The class meeting is one of the best examples we have of this tension between theology and churchmanship. As Wesley himself observed, the idea of the class was conceived at the Bristol society while they were discussing something altogether different—a building debt, as it happened—and it was adopted as a feature of all the societies primarily because it served an immediate need. This was typical of Wesley's leadership of the Methodist movement. He was always open to practical measures to meet the exigencies of a given situation, provided they worked. But they were not adopted thoughtlessly. There had to be nothing against them in scripture, and they were always in keeping with his theological understanding of the church.

The Tension of Wesley's Churchmanship

Fundamental to Wesley's churchmanship was his English Protestant heritage. As an Anglican, he affirmed the validity and authority of the visible church, but he was also influenced by the Puritan concept of the gathered church, based on scripture alone. Wesley emphasized both concepts. He acknowledged the validity of a gathered community, elected by God for a purpose. But this did not negate the wider concept of an inclusive and visible church, reaching out to all, firmly in and of the world, a means of God's prevenient grace.

The phrase which best describes this view of the church comes out of German pietism: *ecclesiola in ecclesia,* the little church in the big church. Wesley found that the *ecclesiola,* the little church, was a self-evident reality among the people to whom he ministered in the Methodist societies. Clearly these groups had been gathered together by God, and blessed with power and purpose. Yet he felt it was important to keep them firmly within the visible Church of England, grounded in the mainstream of the Christian tradition. As long as he lived, he regarded them as valid only insofar as they were part of the larger church, the *ecclesia*. As Frank Baker's definitive study makes clear, Wesley had not the slightest intention of founding a new denomination. His avowed purpose was not "to form the plan of a new church," but to reform the old one.[5] Moreover, this remained his purpose to the end of his ministry. As we know, he approved ordinations for America in 1784, and from 1785 onwards for Scotland. But he still resisted separation of the English societies from the Church of England as an unnecessary schism. In the various sets of rules which constituted Methodist polity, the emphasis was on discipleship within the church, not doctrinal disputes which might divide it.

Even so, the very nature of the societies as "little churches" created an inherent separatist tendency in the movement; and paradoxically, the chief reason for this was Wesley's insistence that the purpose of the church be given priority over its function. He saw the true meaning of discipleship as the *working out* of salvation, and as Methodists took up this commission, becoming living witnesses to their faith, church order and doctrine became less important to him than reaching out to "the tinners in Cornwall, the keelmen in Newcastle, the colliers in Kingswood and Staffordshire, the drunkards, the swearers, the Sabbath-breakers of Moorfield and the harlots of Drury Lane."[6] It was no exaggeration for him to say that he accomplished far more by preaching three days on his father's tomb at Epworth than he had by preaching three years in his pulpit, for his commission was clear:

God in Scripture commands me, according to my power, to instruct the ignorant, reform the wicked, confirm the virtuous. Man forbids me to do this in another's parish: that is, in effect, to do it at all; seeing I have now no parish of my own, nor probably ever shall. Whom then, shall I hear, God or man? . . . *I look upon all the world as my parish*; thus far I mean, that in whatever part of it I am, I judge it meet, right, and my bounden duty to declare unto all that are willing to hear the glad tidings of salvation. This is the work which I know God has called me to do. And sure I am that his blessing attends it.[7]

Wesley was aware that going into the fields with the gospel would be a source of tension between Methodists and the Church of England. Indeed, as the movement gathered momentum, separation from the Church of England in many ways became the most obvious step to take. Anglican critics of Methodism gave every indication that they regarded it as a divisive movement, and would probably have been happy to see it as a separated body. But Wesley's theology always checked the pragmatism of his polity, and he refused to condone or even contemplate separation. He firmly believed that the spirit of Methodism would be seriously hindered by separation from the mother church, and argued strongly for the legitimacy of the Methodist societies within Anglican faith and practice. He pointed out that the purpose of the societies was to encourage members to strengthen each other by talking and praying together as often as possible, practices which were "grounded on the plainest reason, and on so many scriptures both of the Old Testament and New, that it would be tedious to recite them." [8]

The problem was that many of the rank-and-file Methodists did not see it that way, not least because it was possible during the eighteenth century to obtain a license as a dissenting congregation, which gave the right to hold regular Sunday worship services and to have an independent church organization. It seemed unreasonable to many of the societies that Wesley should insist on their remaining part of the Church of England.

He took pains, therefore, to warn the members of the societies against the ill effects of breaking away from the church. The aims of separation, he maintained, were invariably thwarted by the means. "The experiment has been so frequently tried already, and the success has never answered the expectation." [9] Should this occur in Methodism, he noted in 1789, the result would be the dwindling of those who separated into "a dry, dull party." And this, he declared, he would do all in his power to prevent as long as he lived. The essence of his argument was forceful: that separation, if avoidable, merely distracted from the priorities of the faith.

In his sermon *On Schism,* he defined such a step as inherently evil, a grievous breach of the law of love, and contrary to the nature of the faith which ought to unite Christians. Schism, being evil in itself, produced evil fruits, opening a door to uncharitable judgments, to anger and resentment, which in turn led to slandering and back-biting. These were not imaginary results, said Wesley, but plain facts, borne out by events in his own experience. The question was not whether separation *per se* was permissible. Clearly, if a church should lead a member against the scriptures or into some other false teaching, then the member should separate. The sin was *unnecessary* division.[10]

Throughout his ministry, Wesley staunchly upheld this position. It caused more than a few broken relationships with his preachers, and it was never appreciated by the hierarchy of the Church of England. But he saw, in the spirit and the structure of *ecclesiola in ecclesia,* the freedom and accountability for an authentic discipleship, and the significance of giving them equal emphasis. The class meeting was no mere expedient. It was based on a sound and sensitive understanding of the church as the wellspring of faithful Christian living.

For Thought and Discussion

1. Which seemed more important to the early Methodists: faith or works?

2. What do you understand by the phrase "mutual accountability"?

3. What seem to have been Wesley's strengths (a) as a theologian, (b) as a church leader?

4. Can you find examples in the contemporary church of *ecclesiola in ecclesia?*

Chapter Two

Formative Patterns of Discipleship

We can trace a great deal of Wesley's churchmanship to two specific patterns of disciplined Christian living which influenced him during his formative years, each an expression of *ecclesiola in ecclesia:* the Religious Societies of the Church of England, and the communal life of the Moravians.

Practical Piety

The Religious Societies

The Religious Societies had first appeared in the latter part of the seventeenth century, organized through the influence of Dr. Anthony Horneck, a Lutheran minister who had settled in England. They consisted of young men seeking to develop a more disciplined spiritual life, who met together in order to talk about their faith and how they might live it out in the world. Horneck drew up a set of rules, stipulating that they were to "keep close" to the Church of England in all of their meetings, which had a strong liturgical and musical as well as a spiritual emphasis.

Lay leadership was a mark of the Societies from the very beginning. Two "stewards" were appointed to guide the spiritual discussion of each meeting, which was designed to promote the practical aspects of Christian discipleship. Specific questions were put to the members so that everyone's contribution was to the point. According to Josiah Woodward, who wrote the definitive history of the Societies, there was a freedom and openness which enabled the members to speak openly to each other, and to open their hearts in ways which were not possible in other contexts.[11]

By the turn of the century the Societies became increasingly involved in the practical social works of caring for the poor, relieving debt, visiting the sick, providing for orphans, and setting up about a hundred schools in

24

London and the suburbs. Their work further led to the founding of the Society for Promoting Christian Knowledge in 1699, and the Society for the Propagation of the Gospel in Foreign Parts in 1701. Wesley became a corresponding member of the SPCK in August 1732, and must have been familiar with the work of the Societies through his father, Samuel Wesley, who formed one at Epworth in 1701 after reading Woodward's account of their work. Meetings were held on Saturday evenings in order to prepare for the Lord's Day, and membership was restricted to no more than twelve. When more wanted to join—as many as thirty or forty in due course—two members were appointed to start a new society.

This was followed by another significant episode at Epworth. In 1712, while Samuel Wesley was attending the Convocation of the Church of England in London, his wife Susanna began holding what she described as "enlarged family prayers" in the rectory kitchen. During the winter of 1711-12, she had undergone a deep religious experience after reading an account of the work of two Danish Moravian missionaries, and she resolved, even though she was "not a man, nor a minister," to talk more deeply about the faith with those closest to her. She set a time each evening to talk with her children in turn, Thursday being the night for the young John, and she opened the rectory to those neighbors who would come to discuss the "best and most awakening sermons." The numbers in attendance gradually increased, eventually exceeding two hundred. Her use of the word *society* to describe these gatherings cannot have been without significance in view of her husband's previous work. Nor can the gatherings have failed to make a lasting impression on John.[12]

There were many aspects of the Religious Societies which proved to be direct precedents for Methodist polity, perhaps the most important of which were the growing role of lay leadership and involvement in direct social outreach. Their influence can be seen, for example, in the group which Wesley described as the "first rise" of Methodism, the Oxford Holy Club. This was formed by Charles Wesley and two fellow students who wanted to pursue a more diligent spiritual life, and it was an important factor in John's return to Oxford in 1729, when he assumed the role of their spiritual mentor, joining them in their outreach to the poor and imprisoned of the city.

The Religious Societies not only provided precedents for Methodism: in many instances they were its immediate context. Although in decline when the Revival began, they had by no means disappeared, and Wesley was often indebted to them for being receptive to his preaching and for providing his own societies with an important nucleus of membership. Yet there was an important difference. Where Methodism infiltrated a Religious Society, there was a transforming process best described as the liberating *dynamic* of discipleship. Wesley was indebted to the Religious Societies for their disciplined organization, not least because they maintained the structural link with the Church of England which he regarded as crucial for the new Methodist Societies. As the Revival took hold, however, into the disciplined form of the Religious Societies was infused the dynamic of spiritual nurture, a concept of *ecclesiola in ecclesia* which stressed the response of the believer to God's gracious initiatives. And for this, Wesley was indebted to the Moravians.

Communal Piety

The Moravians

The history of the Moravian church can be traced to the radical movements of late medieval Christianity, and in particular the followers of John Hus. Following his execution in 1415, one of the dissident groups to break away from the Roman church named themselves the *Unitas Fratrum,* and held their first synod in 1467. In spite of constant persecution, they continued to grow in strength, and kept alive the "hidden seed" of their fellowship—a concept which they derived from the biblical notion of "remnant." This was of great significance when their tradition was revived by the *Renewed Unitas Fratrum*[13] in the eighteenth century, a tradition which included an episcopacy and a markedly ecumenical perspective.

A further influence on the Moravian church was that of German Pietism, a movement which had begun in the mid-seventeenth century with small house groups organized by a Lutheran pastor, Philipp Jakob Spener, for the purpose of disciplined fellowship. His work was continued by August Hermann Francke, who later became professor of theology at the University of Halle, and under whose leadership Pietism took a more practical turn. An orphan home was established, a charity school, a dispensary and a publishing house; and it is a noteworthy historical link with Wesley's English heritage that Francke took a lively interest in the work of the Anglican Religious Societies, being elected a corresponding member of the SPCK in June 1700.

Most important for the Moravians, however, was the hospitality of the man who was to become their foremost leader, Count Nikolaus Ludwig von Zinzendorf. Zinzendorf grew up within German Pietism, assimilating two of its most important concepts: that of *ecclesiola in ecclesia,* regarded by Spener and Francke alike as a means of reviving the church without occasioning separation; and that of a personal relationship with Christ as the bedrock of the Christian faith. Both were to have profound implications for the new Moravian Church.

In 1722, Zinzendorf bought the estate of Berthelsdorf from his grandmother with the specific intent of creating a haven for refugee Christians of every kind. Hearing of the persecution of the *Unitas Fratrum,* he offered them some land on the estate, and by the end of 1722 a community was established, named *Herrnhut,* "Watch of the Lord." It was organized for the purposes of religious discipline, the members being divided into groups, or *classes,* according to age, sex, and marital status, each with a director chosen by the members themselves. Within these classes there was a mutual oversight for the furtherance of spiritual growth, members being identified as "dead," "awaked," "ignorant," "willing disciples," or "disciples that have made a progress." Similar terminology apears on early Methodist class papers—a language of spiritual discipleship, of dynamic growth rather than inward endeavor.

The initial "classification" of the Herrnhut membership soon developed a twofold division. Groups which were divided according to sex, age, and marital status became known as *choirs,* adopting a residential pattern as the community expanded. At the same time, within the choirs, those who wished to further their spiritual growth formed smaller groups, known as *bands.* These had been a feature of the old *Unitas Fratrum,* and the criterion for membership was spiritual affinity. They consisted originally of only two or three persons, each under the direction of a *band-keeper,* accountable personally to Zinzendorf, and they grew rapidly in number. In 1732 there were 77 bands, and by 1734 they had increased to 100. Their informality provided a degree of flexibility which the choirs did not possess, and Zinzendorf himself was in no doubt as to their significance for the spiritual life of the community. To meet in a band was not merely to exercise self-examination, or to engender a mutual growth in spiritual self-awareness. It was to experience the presence of Christ—a sure and efficacious means of grace.

Early Methodist Piety

Societies and Bands

Wesley's encounter with a group of Moravians en route to America in 1735 and during his time in Georgia was important for two reasons. First of all, it exposed him to their organization of small group fellowship in bands, and convinced him of their value. Their adoption by Wesley in Savannah indicates his positive assessment of their mutual edification as a means of grace; and when, on his return from Georgia in 1738, he was instrumental in forming a Religious Society at the home of the Rev. John Hutton in Fetter Lane, they were adopted along with several other Moravian practices. In the Fetter Lane Society, bands numbered from five to ten persons, who were instructed to share openly with each other their innermost spiritual thoughts and struggles week by week. Wesley kept these groups as an integral part of his polity for the earliest Methodist Societies, drawing up a set of rules for them in 1738, and regarding them as an important subdivision of the membership.

The rules for the bands were very searching, and enjoined on the members to speak "freely and plainly" the true state of their souls, telling of the faults they had committed "in thought, word, or deed," and the temptations they had felt since their last meeting. Moreover, before a person was admitted to a band, they were asked a number of probing questions, such as:

> Have you the forgiveness of your sins?
> Have you peace with God, through our Lord Jesus Christ?
> Is the love of God shed abroad in your heart?
> Do you desire to be told of your faults?
> Do you desire that every one of us should tell you, from time to time, whatsoever is in his heart concerning you?
> Do you desire that, in doing this, we should come as close as possible, that we should cut to the quick, and search your heart to the bottom?

And at every meeting, the following questions were to be asked:

> What known sins have you committed since our last meeting?

What temptations have you met with?
How were you delivered?
What have you thought, said, or done, of which you doubt whether
it be sin or not?

Clearly this was a process of mutual confession; and for those who took their discipleship seriously, as did the members of these early societies, it was a significant point of accountability. At the same time, however, Wesley became aware of the limitations of the bands as a means of grace, and they did not become the basic format for the Methodist movement. There was an intensity to them which did not sit well with many of the people who joined the societies as Wesley and his preachers took to the fields with the gospel. He began to note that, even with this weekly form of mutual confession, many of the members were falling back into old habits, giving Methodism a bad name. And when we read Wesley's account of his visit to Herrnhut in the summer of 1738, we can sense some discomfort with its rarefied atmosphere. In a letter which he wrote (but did not send), he asked the community at Herrnhut whether they were not too much under the influence of Zinzendorf, and thereby were failing to exercise a mature Christian witness in the world.[14]

What was needed for the early Methodist movement was a practical format for the building up of discipleship *in* the world. Most of the people who joined the societies continued with their occupations— servants, farmers, craftsmen, shopkeepers—and therefore had to meet the challenge of Christian witness exactly where they were in the grist and grind of daily living. That Wesley recognized this, and responded to it, was not only a mark of his organizing genius, but also of his deep theological understanding of grace—which, as with his understanding of the church, was likewise an important check on his pragmatism.

For Thought and Discussion

1. What do you regard as the most important contribution of the Religious Societies to the development of early Methodism?

2. What do you find significant about the involvement of the Religious Societies in practical good works?

3. Do you agree that the genius of Wesley's organization of early Methodism was his rejection of the Moravian concept of communal piety?

4. Would you find the mutual confession of the bands helpful for your discipleship? If not, why not?

Chapter Three

Wesley's Understanding of Grace

Christian Assurance and Christian Discipleship

The point at issue between Wesley and the Moravians—and it was sufficiently serious to cause a break in their relationship—was whether the assurance of faith was synonymous with salvation, or whether a sinner could receive forgiveness and reconciliation irrespective of this particular experience. Wesley concluded that salvation was by no means limited to such an assurance. There were certain *means of grace* by which persons could be drawn to God, indeed through which they could seek God. Moreover, once there was a new relationship with God through faith in Christ, these same means of grace were necessary to sustain Christian discipleship and bring it to maturity.

This tells us a great deal about Wesley's view of his ministry and about the structure of the early Methodist societies. In the refined seclusion of Herrnhut, an emphasis on the assurance of faith was part of the disciplined life of the community. It was fostered by the residential choirs and the intimate sharing of the bands. People expected it to happen in their lives, and it did. But in the realities of eighteenth-century England, a doctrine of salvation which depended on experience alone was patently inadequate. This was made clear by the failure of the bands to provide a meaningful source of nurture for the society membership at large. They were designed primarily for persons who were familiar with the life and teachings of the church, and for whom a deep religious experience came largely as an affirmation of all they had hitherto believed and practiced. But for many of those who became Methodists, to join a society meant not only a new faith, but also a new way of life, in which the assurance of salvation came not only from the experience of faith, but also from *living it out.*

To understand how Wesley applied this to the early Methodist societies, we must take a fresh look at his Aldersgate Street experience. Certainly it was a pivotal stage of his Christian pilgrimage, but it was not the only deep religious experience of his life, nor does he seem to have given it the prominence which some of his biographers and disciples have subsequently ascribed to it. Indeed, even in his conversations with the Moravian leader Spangenberg in Georgia—conversations which he himself regarded as crucial in leading up to Aldersgate Street—we find some important guidelines for his later leadership.

"What do you mean by conversion?" Wesley asked. "The passing from darkness to light," replied Spangenberg, "and from the power of Satan unto God." "Is it commonly wrought at once, or by degrees?" "The design of passing thus from darkness unto light is sometimes wrought in a moment, . . . but the passage itself is gradual." "Ought we so to expect the Holy Ghost to convert either our own or our neighbour's soul so as to neglect any outward means?" "Many things are mentioned in Scripture as helps to an entire conversion. So reading the Scripture . . . hearing it . . . fasting . . . self-examination . . . the instructions of experienced persons . . . fervent prayer. None therefore ought to neglect any of these, when it is in their power to use them."[15]

The assurance of faith which Wesley preached and taught was a direct witness of the Spirit of God. Yet it did not preclude accountability to the law of God and to the means of grace. The one followed from the other. The issue was how the doctrine of justification by faith was to be interpreted, and we find that, at the early Conferences which Wesley held with his preachers, a great deal of time was spent on this very question. In 1745, the doctrine was defined in terms of an accountable discipleship. On the one hand, it was grounded in the realities of the visible church—its worship, its sacraments, and its emphasis on practical discipleship in the world, all of which were brought into focus by the Religious Societies. On the other hand, it stressed the evangelical faith of the Moravians, declaring salvation to be received wholly by grace. Together, the two traditions affirmed God's initiative and human response in the immediacy of a new relationship—a relationship *for which the only precondition was a willingness to be open to God's grace.*

Accordingly, God's grace was perceived to be active in the whole range of human experience. It was at work in every human being, preveniently inviting the sinner to reconciliation in a family of love, and creating a tension between the "drawings" of God and the "stifling" or "quenching" of the Spirit by sinful human beings, whose instinct was to resist God's grace. There was a process, therefore, which led to justification, a spiritual searching, a despair, an "emptying" of all self-righteousness, until the human will submitted to God's active grace, and the sinner was justified. Moreover, just as God's prevenient grace invited a sinner to repentance while giving the freedom to resist, so God's sanctifying grace worked a change which the sinner was equally free to resist. The new relationship with God in Christ was always a choice. If the sinner accepted it, then it had to be worked out in the world by an obedient discipleship which transformed the sinner into a new person. But if the choice was *disobedience*, then the new relationship was broken, and could even be destroyed permanently.

Christian Maturity and Christian Obedience

The mark of a mature Christian, therefore, was a consistent obedience to God, in which the new relationship of justifying faith was no longer interrupted by a wayward will, but firmly grounded in a service of love. It was this which Wesley affirmed as the doctrine of Christian perfection: that the inward renewal of the believer could proceed, in this life, to a discipleship in which obedience had become so habitual that the will had lost its tendency to resist God's grace—a point at which faithful discipleship culminated in perfect love, a maturity which was as much a gift of God's grace as everything else in the life of the believer.

With this theological understanding, Wesley discerned a divine immediacy in every moment of Christian discipleship. As he took the gospel the length and breadth of the land, he saw a wide outpouring of grace. He found, in the richness of Methodist religious experience, a spiritual growth that was analogous to birth, childhood, and coming of age. He saw people brought to the critical point of surrender, their lives changed by justifying grace received through faith. When this was maintained in loving obedience, he saw the work of sanctifying grace, leading to the development of religious maturity—a perfection of love which Wesley came to regard as the "second blessing." When this second blessing was taken for granted, however, there was a falling away, even by the most mature. Obedience could not for one moment be neglected.

The critical question for Christian discipleship was how to permit God's grace to foster a maturity of constant obedience, so that sanctifying grace might work with an unimpeded love. It was Wesley's theological understanding of this question which led him to adopt what at first seemed an unbelievably simple solution: a weekly meeting of like-minded persons who would exercise a mutual accountability for their discipleship. This "prudential means of grace" was as profound as it was simple. In adopting the class meeting as the basis for early Methodist polity, Wesley was not only being practical. He was drawing on years of theological searching. The dynamic of early Methodist discipleship was established at the very beginning of the movement on the solid theological principle of justification by faith—how not to resist God's gracious initiatives—and it remains the most important contribution made by Wesley, and by Methodism, to the Christian tradition.

The foundation of Wesley's organization of the Methodist movement lay in his recognition that Christian discipleship was first and foremost *a response to God's grace*, not a striving for virtue or an experience of instant salvation. He could not regard those who did the best they could as beyond the scope of God's salvation any more than he could regard those with the second blessing as beyond sinning. His polity for the Methodist societies took the best of the Anglican Societies and the Moravians alike, and then went further. It affirmed that, while people respond to God's grace at various levels of resistance or acceptance, there are certain Christian practices through which everyone can receive God's grace, regardless of the level of their response. These were the means of grace, ordained by the church and proven in practice. The minutes of the 1744 Conference urged Methodist preachers to use them all, "instituted" and "prudential," and to "enforce the use of them on all persons." The instituted means of grace were listed as prayer (private, family, and public), searching the scripture, the sacrament of the Lord's Supper, fasting, and Christian conference—what today we would call serious conversation about the faith. The prudential means were those personal disciplines and forms of fellowship which helped to ground the Christian in the basics of discipleship.[16]

Christian Fellowship and Christian Accountability

Wesley also understood that people who came to a knowledge of the gospel needed a pattern of spiritual nurture which did not presume a particular religious experience, or a uniform pattern of faith. What was needed initially was a building up of commitment to obedience in the service of Jesus Christ, some form of mutual encouragement and guidance. Thus it was that a Methodist society was defined in its rules as a company of people who, having the form of Godliness, were seeking its power. As Methodist preaching reached those who were not being touched by the church in any other way, so the societies received them with no other condition than that they should *desire* to be saved from their sins. The *General Rules of the United Societies* went on to state, however, that "wherever this [desire] is really fix'd in the soul, it will be shewn by its Fruits," and in order that it "may the more easily be discern'd, whether [the members] are indeed working out their own Salvation, each Society is divided into smaller Companies, called Classes, according to their respective Places of abode."[17]

In other words, the priority of early Methodists was not to seek a particular religious experience, but to pursue an obedient discipleship. Their commitment to the class meeting expressed belief in a salvation which gave them freedom *and* responsibility under God's grace. It was a supportive structure for discipleship, grounded in the realities and the common sense of worldly living; and, as we shall see, it was the muscle of the Methodist movement.

For Thought and Discussion

1. Which is the more important in Wesley's understanding of grace: the assurance of faith or the obedience of discipleship?

2. Do you agree that Christian maturity (Christian perfection) is the development of a constant obedience to God?

3. Wesley regarded the "means of grace" as essential for the seasoned Christian as well as the beginner, or even the enquirer (p. 34). What does this imply for Christian discipleship today?

4. Discuss the statement in the *General Rules* of the Methodist societies, that the members were those who, "having the form of Godliness," were "seeking its power."

Chapter Four

Methodist Discipleship
Mutual Accountability

The Class Meeting

Once he perceived its usefulness and its validity, Wesley adopted the class meeting as the basic structure of Methodism. As we have noted, the idea emerged during a discussion in the Bristol society over the building debt on the New Room. The date was February 15, 1742. The account given us by Wesley states that a retired seaman, known to us only as Captain Foy, proposed that each member of the society should give a penny a week toward clearing the debt. When it was pointed out that a penny a week was beyond the means of many members, he replied that he would personally accept responsibility for collecting the weekly amount from ten or twelve members, and would make up any deficiencies. Others offered to do the same, and so it was agreed to divide the whole society into "little companies, or classes—about twelve in each class," with one person, styled as the leader, to collect the weekly contributions.[18]

What began as a financial expedient soon became an opportunity for pastoral oversight. As Wesley later described it, the class proved to be the very thing that was needed to foster discipleship among the society members. Before long, instead of the leader visiting each member, it was found more convenient for the members to meet as a group, when the leader would not only collect the weekly contributions, but would give advice, reproof, or encouragement. A dynamic of Christian fellowship quickly developed, as members began to be honest with each other, and to help each other in their discipleship.

It is important to remember that the introduction of the class meeting did not bring an end to the bands, which continued alongside the classes for those who needed the more intensive and searching process of mutual confession. But while the bands remained divided according to the Moravian pattern of age, sex, and marital status, the classes were divided pragmatically according to where the members and the leader lived. Men and women, young and old, married and single, all belonged to the class closest to where they lived.

37

The Class Leader

The class leader was a crucial element in a line of authority and communication extending from Wesley to the Methodist membership as a whole, and leaders were given very specific duties in the *General Rules*. While their appointment or removal was the prerogative of himself or his assistants, Wesley was responsive to the dynamics of leadership. He was aware that leaders' authority would depend to a large degree on the respect accorded by the class, not least because they were the ones who exercised accountability for discipleship. They met weekly with the preacher appointed by Wesley as minister of their society, both to report on their members, and themselves to receive advice and instruction. Their selection tended to evolve naturally as societies acknowledged their potential, and the progression from class leader to preacher was not uncommon. By the same token, Wesley and his assistants were quick to discern leadership qualities, and there is little question that they became as skilled a group of spiritual mentors as the church has ever produced.

What Wesley looked for in class leaders was a combination of disciplinary and spiritual discernment, so that fellowship in the classes would be a means of strengthening the discipleship of the members. One of their most important tasks, for example, was to report to the minister if there were those who were disregarding the *General Rules*. There was a good reason for insisting on this strict supervision. In an intimate fellowship, any lack of commitment or discipline on the part of an individual member was bound to be disruptive. If Methodists were to "watch over one another in love," then any member failing to provide this mutual support was certain to be a hindrance.

Wesley further enforced this by introducing a relatively simple procedure which at the same time provided society members with an important symbol of identity: *class tickets*. He adopted them initially at Bristol and Kingswood as a disciplinary measure to guard against "disorderly walkers," some forty of whom were expelled in February 1741. Similar disciplinary action was taken in London the following April, and thereafter he issued tickets to all the societies at a quarterly examination of the classes by himself or one of his preachers. Those who were keeping the society rules were thereby provided with a visible means of encouragement, and at the same time those who were "disorderly" could be removed by withholding their new ticket.

This quarterly examination was a further means of supervising the leaders themselves. As we have noted, they were required to meet weekly with the preacher appointed as their minister to hand in class monies and to give a report on the progress of their members. But an examination of members by the preacher each quarter also provided an important check on how a leader was performing his or her task, as Wesley makes clear at many points in his correspondence. Described as "visitations," the references to them in his journal and diary are myriad. The preachers were constantly directed to be thorough and conscientious in this aspect of their duties, even to the point of visiting door-to-door those who were found not to have been meeting in class.

The leaders were also the initial point of contact for those who wished to join a society. On the recommendation of the leader, a note would be issued for admittance to society meetings, and at the end of the three months the leader would again be consulted about full membership. Just as the class meeting was the occasion of membeship, it was also the condition. Wesley saw the classes as the "sinews" of Methodism, and when a new society was established, the formation of the first class was the immediate priority. Attendance at the weekly meetings was always a condition for the renewal of the quarterly tickets, and preachers were given clear instructions to withhold them from those who were irregular. The general, though unwritten, rule was that three consecutive absences constituted self-expulsion from a class, and leaders were required to keep a record of attendance, as well as to follow up on any absenteeism.

The General Rules

Works of Mercy and Works of Piety

This meant that, once a week, a society member had to give an account of his or her discipleship, and there were two criteria for this accountability. The first was the *General Rules* of 1743, which Wesley never ceased to affirm as the disciplinary framework of Methodism. By keeping them, the spiritual growth of the early Methodists was effected. Without them, it was inevitably impeded. Since there was no prerequisite for Methodist membership other than a desire for salvation, the societies were open to anyone, regardless of their spiritual state. But to continue in membership, there had to be an evidence of their desire for salvation in the doing of outward and visible good works. These were at once a manifestation of faith, and a condition of continuing in it.

Accordingly, members were enjoined to avoid evil, to do no harm, and to do all the good they could for as many as possible. Wesley described these as "Works of Mercy," since they rightly spring from faith, and the Rules give a very detailed list of instructions in this regard. Because the list is so detailed, it provides an interesting comment on eighteenth-century life as well as on Methodist discipleship. But the point it makes is quite seminal—that being a Christian is a matter of living in the world as it is. Discipleship for early Methodists was rooted in *living out* their faith; and while there are items in these Rules which might make us smile, such as the censure of "uncharitable or unprofitable conversation, particularly speaking evil of Magistrates or Ministers," there is little that cannot be readily applied to the late twentieth century. Most certainly we should note the stipulation that, in doing good to their fellow human beings, Methodists should first take care of *bodily* needs—giving food to the hungry, clothes to the naked, visiting or helping those who were sick or in prison. Only then were they instructed to help their souls.

The Rules also enjoined the members of the societies "to attend upon all the Ordinances of God: Such are The publick Worship of God; the Ministry of the Word, either read or expounded; The Supper of the Lord; Private Prayer; Searching the Scriptures; and Fasting, or Abstinence." Wesley regarded these instituted means of grace as "Works of Piety"—those disciplines and practices of the church without which any attempt to pursue Christian discipleship was doomed to failure. It indicates not only that he perceived worldly service in the name of Christ to be ineffectual without the power of the Holy Spirit, but also that the "inner discipline" of Methodism was inexorably linked to that of the Church of England. He developed the polity of small group fellowship on the assumption that the wider questions of doctrine and order were already established. Members of Nonconformist churches who joined the societies were expected to fulfill their congregational obligation no less than parishioners of the Church of England.

Spiritual Growth

Maturity of Obedience

The second criterion for the quarterly renewal of class tickets was a questioning of class members—and leaders—about their spiritual growth. This was not, of course, the sort of intensive questioning which took place in the bands. There were too many variables in a class meeting for that. But spiritual growth was acknowledged to be both the sign and the result of obedient discipleship, and class leaders were asked to note on their records whether a member was still searching for faith ("awakened"), had experienced the new birth in Christ ("justified"), or had become mature in the faith ("gone on to perfection"). Along with the pragmatism of the class meeting format was a sensitivity to the mysteries of grace.[19]

This was further evident in Wesley's concern to prevent the meetings from becoming a mere formality. By their very nature, the classes had a fixed agenda, which at once provided a structure for the meetings and a danger. It is clear from contemporary accounts that the exchanges in the class meetings were almost entirely catechetical between the leader and each member of the group. The process was one of question and answer, with the leader articulating what was felt to be the point which would most profitably be shared by the other members—a method which served to emphasize that the primary purpose of the meeting was for each person to give an account to the others of his or her discipleship. Meetings began with a prayer and a hymn, and then the leader, beginning with him or herself, asked how each member had kept the rules of the societies during the past week, and also what was the state of his or her soul. In response, the leader would give appropriate comments of praise, reproof, or advice.

The danger was that the format of question and answer might become monotonous, thereby stifling the dynamic of fellowship which developed as the class members became better acquainted with each other. Wesley was aware of this potential obstacle, and advised class leaders not only to vary the pattern of their question, but also to pursue the individual spiritual progress of the members as a means of discerning how God was at work in their lives. Once the basic guidelines for discipleship were being fulfilled, the purpose of the group was to share in the realities of one another's pilgrimage, and thereby in their growth to spiritual maturity.

Needless to say, spiritual maturity was even more the agenda for band meetings, in which there was a much more informal exchange. They experienced a greater intimacy, due in large part to Wesley's restriction of membership to those who wanted and needed "some means of closer union." It was here that the spiritual quest for perfection was fostered and guided, band members being subjected to more rigorous disciplinary supervision than the classes. The preachers were instructed to meet with them weekly, and to be especially vigilant in enforcing the Rules. Members received specially designated class tickets, which were granted only after a trial period of three months, thereby distinguishing them as those who were committed to the quest for Christian maturity.

The class meeting, however, remained the basic unit of Methodist organizational structure, and was also the most effective means of spiritual nurture for the membership as a whole. All Methodists, whether or not they were meeting in band, had to meet once a week with their class to give an account of their discipleship. It was an inclusive requirement, and it was an affirmation of grace. The "path to perfection" began *and continued* with an accountability for the basics of Christian discipleship, without which no genuine progress could be made in the Christian life. It must now be asked whether it continues to offer the church of today a paradigm for discipleship.

For Thought and Discussion

1. Do you think that the role of the early Methodist class leader is one which could prove useful in the church today? In what ways?

2. The class ticket was a means of quietly removing inactive society members from the rolls. Would this be practicable for the local congregation today? If not, why not?

3. The weekly class meeting was a point of accountability for the early Methodists. Why do you think it is no longer a requirement for church membership?

4. Which seems to have been more important for the early Methodist societies: the band or the class meeting? Why?

Chapter Five

The Class Meeting
for Today

The Call to Commitment

We began this study with the observation that Christians today are looking for ways in which to make their faith more meaningful. Yet the quest for a deeper spiritual commitment which pervades the American church seems rarely to produce a more obedient discipleship. There are many who wish to reject the option of a lukewarm folk religion, which demands little of the believer, and offers all sorts of personal benefits the church was never meant to provide—with an appalling wear and tear on its human and material resources. At the same time, they are uncomfortable with a radical Christian witness which seems to present impossible demands—and which raises serious questions about the extent to which it is a witness of grace.

We also observed that these tensions are by no means new. Christians have been confronted by the challenge of their witness in every age, and there have never been easy answers. The truth of the matter is that it has always been difficult to sustain a faithful Christian witness in the world, and for a very simple reason: the world is not yet the kingdom of God. Sin is still rampant, and a sinful world will always resist the coming New Age of Jesus Christ. In this regard, the late twentieth century is no different from any other time.

The purpose of looking at our Methodist heritage, therefore, has been to ask how our forebears met this challenge in another day and age. Some of the problems they faced are strikingly similar to our own. There was tremendous social upheaval as the early industrial revolution began to uproot people from the countryside and overcrowd the cities. This was accompanied by economic uncertainty, and areas of abject poverty. Needless to say, all of this produced a wave of crime. The response was a penal code, the conditions of which we would regard today as savage, but the demands for which are all too familiar.

43

Social factors, however, are not the only or even the major occasion of our sense of identification with the early Methodists. What links us is the oneness of the Holy Spirit, making us closer to them in the faith than we are to contemporary neighbors who do not share our understanding of the gospel. Since it is ultimately impossible to correlate the eighteenth century with our own time, what we must ask in our study of their discipleship is how they found the strength to live their lives as Christians. We must ask how they were sustained, and whether the source of the strength with which they met the challenges of their day can help us in our witness to the twentieth century world.

Accountability in the Class Meeting

If we look at the class meeting as the sinews which held the early Methodist movement together, five aspects emerge as being particularly important for the members of the societies:

1. It was a point of accountability for Christian discipleship.

The key to understanding the dynamic of the early class meeting is the word *accountability*. As we have noted, the members developed an openness to one another, and an intimacy which permitted them to share their spiritual pilgrimage unreservedly. But it is a mistake to assume that the class meeting was essentially an intensive group experience, or even primarily a means of spiritual growth. These were benefits which followed from the *first* priority of the weekly meeting, which was to "watch over one another in love." If we emphasize the love which they shared to the exclusion of the mutual accountability which they exercised, both for the means of grace and for the obedience of their discipleship, we seriously misunderstand the purpose and the function of their meetings.

The *General Rules* of 1743 put it well. Methodists were those who, "having the Form, and seeking the Power of Godliness, united in order to pray together, to receive the Word of Exhortation, and to watch over one another in Love, that they may help each other to work out their Salvation."

2. It was a point of accountability for the means of grace.

John Wesley knew the central importance of the means of grace for a committed discipleship, and listed them for the early Methodists in the *General Rules:* daily prayer, daily reading of the scriptures, regular worship, frequent sacrament of Holy Communion, temperance and fasting, Christian conversation, and meeting in Christian fellowship to "watch over one another in love." Of all these, Wesley regarded the last as perhaps the most important. Indeed, he regarded solitary Christianity as a contradiction in terms, and he constantly warned the members of the societies that they took a grave risk with their discipleship if they did not use this "prudential means of grace." Regular attendance at the weekly class meeting was an absolute requirement.

3. It was a point of accountability for living in the world.

There were many small group movements in Wesley's day, and many aspects of the Evangelical Revival were seemingly more successful than his. But Methodism prevailed because the bedrock of the early societies was an active witness *in the world.* These Methodists did not seek pleasant surroundings on weekends in order to "find God." They knew that God had found them right where they were. The Methodist classes had nowhere else to meet but where the members lived and worked. And they gathered week by week because they knew that, when the prayer was given and the hymn was sung, God was present in the power of the Holy Spirit, and was there to bless.

Moreover, they knew that when they resumed their "daily round and common task," God would be there ahead of them. Far from running away from the world, the class meeting helped the early Methodists to view their surroundings in a new light. By grace, they had the eyes to see. And they needed grace—how they needed it! For to be a Methodist was to be a marked person, subject to ridicule, disdain, persecution, and frequently personal assault. To live out a Methodist witness in the crowded urban areas which were so rapidly spreading in eighteenth century England, or in the villages with their tight community life, was to be under scrutiny at every turn. The words of the hymn, which Charles

Wesley wrote for them, take on new meaning when we remember what
they faced:

> Forth in Thy Name, O Lord, I go,
> My daily labour to pursue,
> Thee, only Thee, resolved to know,
> In all I think, or speak, or do.[20]

4. It was a point of accountability to and for the church.

Because Wesley insisted that the Methodist societies remain within
the Church of England, the class meeting became a twofold point of
churchly accountability. First of all, it held the members of the classes
accountable *to* church discipline. They were committed to availing
themselves of the instituted means of grace, those ordinances of the
church through which grace might be received, and listed, as we have
noted, in the *General Rules* of the societies.

But at the same time, the class meeting was a point of accountability
for the church. The Methodists were actually doing what the church
instructed faithful Christians to do, but which most parishioners and
many clergy had failed to do for years—if ever they had. It was this
which Wesley regarded as one of the most important reforming influences of the Methodist movement: a calling back of the church to the
principles of scriptural Christianity, to personal holiness and to social
responsibility, through its own ordinances.

5. It was a point of accountability to the Holy Spirit.

Accountability to and for the church left the Methodist societies and
classes free in turn to respond to the promptings of the Spirit as they
took their message and their witness the length and breadth of the land.
By affirming the structure of the large church, the *ecclesia*, Methodism
functioned as a collection of little churches, *ecclesiolae*. Thus they were
unencumbered by churchly responsibilities,and were able to pursue an
active discipleship in the world.

Without this structural relationship to the Church of England, which Wesley constantly endeavored to foster, the societies might indeed have been vulnerable to the charges of "enthusiasm" which were leveled at them, and which Wesley was at such pains to resist. Instead, the genius of the movement was that it did not matter what sort of religious experience people had received—or whether they had received an experience at all. What counted was a willingness to join with others of like purpose in living out an obedient discipleship in the world. Growth in grace, the new birth, and gift of the "second blessing," all of these followed. But to develop and sustain a living faith, they knew that first they had to develop an obedience to the Spirit of God, many of whose guidelines for daily living required disciplined application rather than a special experience.

In these five ways, the class meeting helped the early Methodists exercise accountability for their faith. It must now be asked whether it can help us in our discipleship today.

Accountability in the Church Today

Eighteenth century England cannot be transferred to twentieth century North America. For that matter, nor can it be transferred to twentieth century England! But it may be possible to *transplant* the essence of the class meeting into our time, allowing for the difference between early and contemporary Methodism, allowing also for new shoots to grow from the soil of a different age. The movement which began with the Wesley brothers is now two hundred years old as a church. As we shall see, this has some profound implications for how we view the early class meeting as a paradigm for our discipleship; and perhaps the best way to consider this is to examine the relevance today of the same five points of accountability.

1. Accountability for Christian Discipleship

Of all the "common sense" virtues of the class meeting, this is the most important. We know what it is like to be around people whose schedule runs like clockwork, whose homes are immaculate, who seem to find their work effortless, and who are always, infuriatingly, correct. There is an aura of unreality about them. They seem to be superhuman, in a league altogether different from ours. Because for most of us, the only way to form personal disciplines is to join with others of like purpose, and make ourselves mutually accountable for doing them. There is no secret recipe for success in this. It is just practical common sense.

If we look around us, we can see that this approach is widely used today. We noted some examples in the Introduction, and others immediately come to mind. People who wish to exercise together will play tennis. People who wish to sharpen their understanding of a subject will discuss it together. People who wish to renovate a house or repair a car will call on neighbors to help them. And who wishes to go to a ball game or a concert alone? But the two clearest examples of mutual accountability are Alcoholics Anonymous and Weight Watchers. These groups are made up of people who face a common problem, have acknowledged it, and have agreed to help one another resist it. They will never say they have *overcome* the problem, for an alcoholic and a compulsive eater remain that way for the rest of their lives. They can reach a point, however, where they *sustain a resistance* to their problem; and by living one day at a time, they can achieve a moment-by-moment victory.

So it is with those of us who call ourselves Christians. Our problem? We are sinners. And sinners we shall remain until our salvation in Christ Jesus has been brought to fulfillment in the New Age. But we are *forgiven* and *reconciled* sinners, accepted by God *just as we are.* And once forgiven and reconciled, we grow in grace to the extent we are obedient in our discipleship. The choice is always ours, as is the choice of how best to be obedient to grace. The early Methodists discovered how to do this, and their method is as relevant today as it was two hundred years ago. And why not—we are still called *Methodists!*

2. Accountability for the Means of Grace

It is an understandable mistake of many Christians to assume that their own faith experience is unique. To do this is to fall prey to the temptation to become little "pockets of grace," expecting special treatment from God irrespective of the grace imparted to other Christians. In one sense, of course, this is true. God deals with each of us individually. But our Christian experience is not unique. We share the faith with countless Christians today; and, more significantly, we share it with countless others who have preceded us on this pilgrimage across the centuries. Their wisdom has established that there are ways in which we can receive grace from God—means of grace, which have come to us through the tradition of the church.

The message of the scripture is that God looks upon us as a family, with family rules by which to abide (Romans 12; 1 Corinthians 12). And the family rules of the church are these means of grace. If we are not availing ourselves of them—and a quick check in the average congregation usually shows that we are not—then clearly we need to commit ourselves to a method of accountability. For without grace to sustain us in our task, our relationship with God becomes increasingly self-serving, a mere projection of ourselves and our desires.

3. Accountability for Living in the World

The center of the Christian faith is that God became a human being. We frequently overlook the significance of this for our discipleship, though the early Methodists did not. They lived it, they sang about it, and they proclaimed it throughout the land. Because God had become a human being, they knew that the world was acceptable to God, and worth saving from its evil. Because God became a human being, the human race was acceptable to God and worth saving from its sin. Because God came as a servant to the human race, faithful Christians were called to follow that example in service to the world. To live faithfully in the world was no more than to seek Christ where he was to be found.

Christians should be suspicious of any activity which suggests that a retreat from the world is the way to God. Yes, we all need relaxation and recreation—but God is no more nor less present at those times than in the daily grist and grind of our work and in the familiar nooks and crannies of our homes. "I Found It!" we used to read on bumper stickers. On the contrary, it is God who finds us, *wherever* we are.

4. Accountability to and for the Church

When we seek to apply the principles of the class meeting to contemporary Methodism, we should remember one very important change that has taken place since Wesley's day. Methodism has become a church, at once inclusive and pluralistic. It is now itself the big church, within which we must expect little churches to emerge in varying forms and with varying purposes. Just as Methodism was not unique as a little church in its early days, so the little churches in the contemporary Methodist church will find a range of expressions, from the Sunday school class to the house Bible study group, to cells for social action.

The question, therefore, is how the particular expression of the *ecclesiola* in the early class meeting can be transplanted into contemporary Methodism while affirming an accountability to the larger church, the *ecclesia,* which is now also Methodist. It means, first of all, that by no means everyone will be ready to join such a group, any more than every member of the Church of England was ready to become a Methodist in Wesley's day. Christian commitment, as the early Methodists acknowledged, was not a case of either/or, but a growth in faith *toward* a deeper commitment. There are going to be those in every church who have advanced in their faith journey to a point of maturity where the challenge to discipleship has come in a new and forceful way. There are going to be those, on the other hand, whose pilgrimage has not yet brought them to this point—and the church must be accepting of both.

It also means that those who *are* ready to join such groups should accept the necessity of the large church within which to make their deeper commitment. Just as those who wish to become mutually accountable for their discipleship should not be disdainful toward those who do not feel ready for such a step, so should those who are not ready for this deeper commitment feel threatened by those who are.

5. Accountability to the Holy Spirit

Wesley's concept of grace as he applied it through the early Methodist class meeting can be expressed quite simply: There are no limits to God's gracious initiatives. Indeed, the ultimate gift of God's grace is the freedom to resist it, and thus the freedom to surrender to it. It is precisely this freedom which makes the role of common sense so pivotal in our journey of faith. If the grace of God is the way to forgiveness and reconciliation, and if God is willing to accept us sinners just as we are, then it is only common sense to do the best we can to receive God's grace.

It is this distinctive characteristic of the early class meeting which, when all else is considered, merits our commitment today. Whenever Christians meet together in the name of Christ, they will, as we recognize from our modern knowledge of group dynamics, engender a warmth and intimacy. But something else will happen. The Spirit of God will also be present, working in and through the dynamics, to empower them in service for the coming New Age of Jesus Christ.

This is why Christians the world over are drawn to such fellowship as the source of their spiritual strength. It is a scriptural promise that Christ will be in the midst of those who gather in his name, a promise claimed and honored in the richness of *koinonia* from the earliest days of the church. In the sharing of insights and hopes, of discouragements and defeats, of joys and victories, of temptations and weaknesses, of strengths and accomplishments, of the burdens of injustice and the hopes of liberation, Christians find the bedrock of their faith. At each stage of their journey, they find the grace of God more sustaining, and lose themselves more profoundly in the will of God.

The Call to Costly Discipleship

This spiritual strength is understood best of all by Christians who live in a context of repression, be it social, economic, or political—in First, Second, or Third World. When obedience to Christ is a matter of choosing between social acceptance and persecution, between economic security and impoverishment, between political freedom and captivity or torture, and even between life and death, then witness indeed is a work of grace. If there is resentment on the part of Christians elsewhere in the world about the seeming indifference of the Western church to the realities of costly discipleship, it does not lie in a censure of the freedom and wealth of an affluent society. It lies rather in their inability to understand how Christians in one part of the world regard the Christian faith as a source of personal fulfillment, when witness elsewhere in the world is unavoidably sacrificial, and so utterly dependent on grace. They find it quite incomprehensible that the fellowship

and vitality of small groups should be used for *anything* other than
obedience to the Holy Spirit. Because those who take seriously the
command of Christ to identify with the poor and needy, and whose
witness often demands that they leave the security of the large church to
form little churches in marginal fringes of society, know better than
anyone that their discipleship must be grounded in the realities of
enabling grace.

Perhaps it is for this reason, most of all, that the call to accountable
discipleship comes to us today in North America. Our brothers and
sisters in the world church are "watching over us in love," reminding us
of our responsibilities as members of the Body of Christ. And in our own
Methodist tradition, we have the answer: the class meeting.

An Echo of the Class Meeting

Fortunately there are still some echoes of it to be found in Methodism,
and in this regard I take the liberty of recounting a personal story. As a
young local preacher on trial in the North of England some twenty-five
years ago, I was invited to address the mid-week meeting at a small
Methodist chapel in a coal-mining village. The street was narrow, curv-
ing down from the main road on a sharp incline, and was dimly lit by
gas lamps. It was late fall, and the evening was chilly and damp, a light
mist enveloping the small stone building as the people gathered in the
annex which served as a meeting place. Cold and unwelcoming at first,
the room began to fill with the warmth of Christian fellowship as people
arrived and greeted one another—though no one spoke without first
bowing for a moment of silent prayer. The opening hymn was followed
by a prayer, a scripture reading, and then by more hymns, as the
organist, who had to pump with his feet, found his second wind. After
several choruses of favorite selections, he assumed his place among the
rest of us, forehead glistening.

The leader of the meeting then took over, dominating the proceed-
ings with a natural authority. He was a coalminer, standing tall and erect
with the stiffness of those who spend their working hours bent double
underground. He welcomed everyone by name, addressing each in
turn with informal yet discerning remarks. Each of his comments was
received unquestioningly by the person concerned, including several
rebukes: for not attending meetings regularly ("we meet here *every*

week, you know"); for missing Sunday worship ("we'd all like to lie in of a morning, so *that's* no excuse"); for being overheard using bad language at the coalmine ("people know you come here to chapel, and that makes a bad witness"); and for having an argument in the choir before worship last Sunday evening ("anyone could see what had been going on when you people came out to sing").

But he also had words of praise and encouragement for those who had witnessed to their faith or who had been especially helpful in the community—words which in some instances were a surprise to the person concerned, and all of which drew sympathetic murmurs of appreciation from the rest of the gathering. One person had organized a fund-raising march for the mentally disabled; another had been awarded a certificate of recognition for service to the local branch of the Red Cross; another had been commended privately to the leader for his role at a recent meeting of the coalminers' Trade Union. Each received a word of praise in turn, but the praise was not lavish. Clearly they had done no more than was expected of good Methodists.

Throughout these remarks, the guidance and instruction of the leader were accepted unquestioningly, and his credentials have become clearer to me as the years have passed. Those who were rebuked gave the impression that they would have been disappointed had they not been called to task. Those who were praised and encouraged showed that they did not accept it as a personal congratulation, but rather as a token of their contribution to the witness of the chapel as a whole. It was, to coin a phrase, a good coaching session, and as I was given the lectern to deliver my message, I knew that the audience was as discerning as any I was ever likely to address. Spiritually, they were well attuned; and in terms of Christian obedience, they were seasoned. Moreover, they were hungry for one thing only—the authentic word of the gospel to sustain them in their task. Anything else would have been a waste of their time.

This was not a class meeting in the form that the early Methodists knew it, but it was an echo loud and clear. The dynamic was mutual accountability, persons helping one another to render their discipleship more effective. There was a common task, a perceived challenge, and thus a need for mutual support. Their concern was not to grow in spiritual perception. That would have been to put the cart before the horse. Their objective was rather to hold fast to the grace they were already receiving—to permit the strength and the love of God to flow through their lives unimpeded. They wanted to be obedient to the promptings of a God who was active in their lives, but who could still be resisted if they succumbed to any of the temptations or pressures of the world in which they lived and worked. So they came together because they needed each other. Without this accountability, without this obedience, there could be no growth; but with it, growth would follow as surely as a plant grows from a nurtured seed. They had their priorities correctly in order at that meeting; they knew the importance of an accountable discipleship.

A Renewed Call to Commitment

This same understanding of grace and accountability can be a means of furthering the call to discipleship in our own day and age, and it is time to outline a model for its application in the local church: *Covenant Discipleship Groups*. As the model is unfolded, many similarities with the early class meeting will be observed, but also some significant differences. It is designed to affirm on the one hand the validity of the larger *ecclesia* and the means of grace which it affords, and on the other hand to acknowledge the authenticity of the *ecclesiola*, through which the grace of God calls the faithful disciple to ever-deepening levels of commitment. It does not preclude other forms of group activity in the life and work of the church, but rather provides a very particular format for the *basics* of Christian discipleship—and an accountability for the means of grace in the power of the Holy Spirit.

As Wesley has made clear to us, the Christian faith is rarely experienced as growth, even though growth does take place and is to be expected. Faithful discipleship lived out under God's sovereign grace is above all a matter of *holding fast*. It is doing the best one can with the gifts one has received, in the freedom and responsibility of joyful obedience. Covenant Discipleship Groups are for those who wish to share in that endeavor.

For Thought and Discussion

1. On page 48, the format of the class meeting is likened to that of Alcoholics Anonymous or Weight Watchers. Discuss.

2. Do you agree that Methodists today are neglecting the means of grace (page 49)? How often, for example, should we take the sacrament of Holy Communion?

3. "Christians should be suspicious of any activity which suggests that a retreat from the world is the way to God" (page 49). Discuss.

4. What do you perceive to be the importance of (a) the *ecclesia*, the large church; and (b) the *ecclesiola*, the little church?

5. Small groups are widespread in the contemporary North American church. In the light of the early class meeting, how many of these groups should be re-examined for their true purpose?

6. Have there been any "echoes" of the early class meeting in your own Christian pilgrimage?

Part Two

Covenant Discipleship Groups

A Covenant Discipleship Group consists of two to seven people who agree to meet together for one hour per week in order to hold themselves mutually accountable for their discipleship. They do this by affirming a written covenant on which they themselves have agreed.

Chapter Six

The Formation of Covenant Discipleship Groups

1. Introducing the Idea to the Congregation

Membership in a Covenant Discipleship Group is vocational.

It should be noted at the outset that by no means every member of a local church will wish to make a commitment to a Covenant Discipleship Group. The reason is simple: By no means everyone is ready to do so. If this seems surprising, given the fact that the disciplines are quite minimal, then it must be remembered that, according to the catholicity and inclusiveness of Wesley's doctrine of grace, people respond to God's initiatives with varying degrees of commitment. There is nothing in the covenant of discipleship which a person does not promise to be and to do when joining the church; but the extent to which this commitment is lived out will depend on the stage of a person's faith—i.e., the extent to which he or she responds to God's grace.

When covenant groups have been introduced to local churches, it has been found that those who make the commitment to join a group comprise more or less 15 percent of the worshiping congregation.

This does not mean, however, that an opportunity to join a covenant group should not be given regularly to all church members. The seminal work which has been done in the area of faith development by James W. Fowler is directly affirming of Wesley's remarkable understanding of religious vocation: that it is progressive, with each stage having its own integrity.[21] It follows that church members will wish to

59

make a deeper commitment to their faith at certain points in their pilgrimage, and should feel free to do so in the environment of their local church. Covenant groups have proved to be an excellent way of keeping such a vocational step constantly available, providing the opportunity to extend the invitation, not only to discipleship, but to *further* discipleship.

The role of the minister is pivotal.

The minister of a church is the first person who must be convinced of the value and validity of covenant discipleship groups if they are to be introduced into a local congregation. This is not to imply that the groups require intensive pastoral supervision. On the contrary, one of their strengths is that they quickly become self-supervising and self-generating. But if they are to be integral to the life and work of a church, the minister must be certain of their function in relation to everything else that constitutes its ministry and mission—precisely why the theology which undergirds the concept is so important.

By the same token, if the minister of a church is not convinced of the validity of covenant groups, there is little likelihood of their ever being effectively adopted by a congregation.

Through preaching, through pastoral care, through the countless private conversations and public exchanges in which a minister shares, the concept of covenant groups can be introduced as a call to commitment. It is a call which many church members wish to hear, and to which they are ready to respond. Fifteen percent of the worshiping congregation may not be a majority, but the figure has proved to be quite consistent in a wide range of local church contexts, and it is by no means an insignificant number.

2. The Pilot Group

It is best to begin with a pilot group.

By far the most effective way of introducing Covenant Discipleship Groups to a congregation is through a pilot group, and for several reasons:

a.) The pilot group is a good preparation for the program. It provides a source of leadership and expertise when the groups are introduced to the congregation as a whole.

b.) The pilot group is an effective way of making people aware of the concept of Covenant Discipleship. By the time a pilot group has been meeting for several months, word will have spread through the church. Questions will have been raised and answered, with increased expectancy of the time when membership is to be opened to everyone.

c.) A pilot group does not place an undue administrative burden on the minister and church staff. Between the formation of the pilot group and the opening of the groups to the membership at large, there is ample time to prepare for the logistics of wider participation.

d.) The pilot group is able to explore the format of Covenant Discipleship on behalf of the church membership without the pressure of success or failure. There are some pitfalls—the "Doldrums," for example (see p. 111)—and it is helpful to have the freedom to encounter high and low points as an exploratory exercise.

The pilot group(s) should be formed with care.

The best pilot groups are those which can be formed by persons who are genuinely interested in this sort of a commitment. It is important, however, not to give the impression that Covenant Discipleship is an exclusive activity. A low-key announcement should be made, from the pulpit or in the Sunday bulletin, that the program is being considered for adoption in the congregation, and that the first step is the formation of a pilot group. Interested persons should be invited to contact the pastor or the church office.

In all probability, there will have to be a number of direct invitations to make up the membership of the pilot group. But should there be more volunteers than are needed, it is possible to form a second, or even a third pilot group—though no more than three.

Pilot groups, as with all Covenant Discipleship groups, should have a limit of seven members. If an eighth person wishes to join, then two groups of four should be formed, etc., up to the maximum of three groups.

Participation of the minister and church staff is important.

The pivotal role of the minister has already been noted in the introduction of Covenant Discipleship groups to the congregation. By the same token, participation of the minister in the pilot group is extremely important. In larger churches, this includes associate pastors, diaconal ministers, and other staff members. If one pilot group is formed, participation may be delegated to an associate; though it should be noted that in a multiple-staff church there is the opportunity for two or three pilot groups, each with staff participation.

Unless a lay person in the pilot group has some expertise in group dynamics, it is usually helpful for the minister or staff member to assume the role of leader for several weeks. This is explored in more detail in Chapter Eight.

3. Writing the Covenant

When the pilot group is formed, the first task is to draw up the covenant which will be the basis for its weekly meetings. This is a covenant of intent, consisting of a number of clauses which express the resolve of the members to carry out certain agreed disciplines. It is also a covenant of grace, with introductory and concluding statements which ground it in God's saving righteousness.

Preamble and Conclusion

The preamble and conclusion to the covenant give the members of the group an opportunity to express their openness to the grace of Jesus Christ, and their resolve to pursue an obedient discipleship.

They may wish to adopt the preamble and conclusion from the sample covenant on page 64; or they may wish to draft their own, in which case several weekly meetings may be needed before they agree on the exact wording.

The group should take as long as necessary in the writing of the covenant. It will be the touchstone of their accountability, and should be a document which each member can wholeheartedly affirm as a statement of faith and intent.

Clauses of the Covenant

Required Clauses

The required clauses are those which correspond to the three emphases of the early Methodist *General Rules*: Avoiding Evil; Doing Good; and Using the Means of Grace. Though these are drafted in language which can be appropriated by late twentieth-century Christians, the content remains the same.

Optional, or Contextual Clauses

The optional, or contextual, clauses are added at the discretion of the group members, so that each person can appropriate the covenant with a full sense of ownership and participation. These clauses provide a great deal of flexibility and creative response in the weekly meetings.

A Sample Covenant of Discipleship

This covenant illustrates the preamble, conclusion, and required
clauses commonly used in Covenant Discipleship groups.
Examples of optional clauses are found on the following pages.

Knowing that Jesus Christ died that I might have eternal life, I herewith pledge myself to be his disciple,
holding nothing back, but yielding all to the gracious
initiatives of the Holy Spirit. I faithfully pledge my time,
my skills, my resources, and my strength, to search out
God's will for me, and to obey.

*I will obey the promptings of the Holy Spirit to
serve God and my neighbor.
I will heed the warnings of the Holy Spirit not to
sin against God and my neighbor.
I will worship each Sunday unless prevented.
I will receive the Sacrament of Holy Communion
each week.
I will pray each day, privately, and with my family
or friends.
I will read and study the Scriptures each day.
I will prayerfully care for my body and for the
world in which I live.
I will share in Christian fellowship each week
where I will be accountable for my discipleship.*

I hereby make my commitment, trusting in the grace of God
to work in me that I might have strength to keep this
covenant.

Date: _____ Signed: _____

Optional Clauses

The only guideline to follow in this regard is that all optional clauses should in fact be practicable, both to attempt and to sustain. The principle of the covenant groups is the acknowledgment that God's gracious initiatives reach people where they are in the world, and that men and women can respond to them within the routines of daily living. The essence of the spirituality practiced in the early Methodist class meetings was that the Christian does not have to withdraw from the world, permanently or temporarily, to be in communion with God. The discipline comes in learning not to resist the gracious initiatives of God's Spirit in their immediate worldly setting.

Groups should therefore feel free to introduce optional clauses for a limited time if need be, or to drop clauses which no longer require accountability. Changing membership of a group, for example, is often a factor in determining "contextual" clauses, such as:

I will prayerfully plan my study time.

(From the covenant of a group of college students.)

I will spend an hour each day with my children.

(From the covenant of a group of young married couples.)

I will be honest in all things at my place of work.

(From the covenant of a group of office workers.)

I will offer friendship each day to someone of an ethnic background different from my own.

(From the covenants of a number of groups, with members ranging from suburban women to farm workers and inner-city unemployed.)

I will witness to my faith in Christ at least once each day.

(From the covenant of a group in a state prison.)

Relevance and Specificity

As the process of accountability comes into focus, group members may also wish to make the required clauses more specific, in order to be more relevant to their respective patterns of discipleship. Again, these should be introduced as and when necessary. For example:

I will eat one less meal each day, and give the money to feed the hungry.

When I am aware of injustice to others, I will not remain silent.

I will spend at least one hour each day helping someone in need.

I will give four hours each week to furthering the cause of the disadvantaged in my community.

I will keep a diary to plan my daily and weekly prayers.

I will record the spiritual insights of my daily Bible reading.

I will partake of the sacrament of Holy Communion each day.

I will be faithful in my stewardship of God's resources.

I will return to God at least a tenth of all that I receive.

I will seek the guidance of the Holy Spirit in fasting.

Prioritizing

In making the final selection of optional clauses, it must be remembered that the required clauses of the covenant have priority, and that in many instances the individual responses to these questions during the catechetical process of the group will address the issues of relevance and specificity alike. Only when the group is agreed that each member wishes to be accountable for an optional clause should it be added.

Open Clauses

In the event of disagreement over optional clauses, it is possible to add an open clause to the covenant, in which each member agrees to be accountable for some aspect of discipleship of particular importance to himself or herself. The proviso here is that the nature of the accountability must be declared to the group at the close of the preceding meeting, and the member be asked at the following meeting whether or not the clause was fulfilled. It is unlikely that members of a new group will feel sufficiently at ease to opt for open clauses. It may be several months before such commitments are undertaken by a group—and then usually as a point of growth in their mutual accountability.

Length of the Covenant

The number of clauses in a covenant has no fixed limit, but should be governed by the ability of a group to go through each clause with each member in one hour. In practice, therefore, a covenant should probably contain no more than ten clauses in all; though if group members feel it important to add clauses in order to be fully accountable for their discipleship, they should feel free to do so. (See "The Form of the Meeting," p. 72.)

Signing the Covenant

Once the covenant is agreed, someone in the group should accept responsibility for having it reproduced in a convenient format. Bulletin-insert size (8½" by 5½") is convenient and can be folded into a wallet or purse. There should be room for a date and signature; and, when it has been reproduced for each member of the group, the first step at the next meeting should be to have everyone sign a copy.

4. Commitment to the Group

Mutual Accountability

When the covenant is signed by the members of the group, it should be stressed that their commitment is being made indefinitely. This is not a group activity to be tried for a period, nor is it subject to feelings of personal fulfillment. It is to be a "watching over one another in love," and covenant groups cannot function unless this mutual accountability is understood by all members at the outset.

Unavoidable absences should be intimated to the group in advance, or excused as soon as possible afterwards. If a member is absent without an explanation, someone from the group should undertake to contact that person to indicate that he or she was missed by the others.

Leaving the Group

It should further be made clear when the covenant is signed that the only valid reason for leaving a group is a strong sense of vocation that the commitment of one's discipleship can be better fulfilled in other ways. If a member reaches such a decision prayerfully, then departure from the group should be intentional, shared with the other members in a meeting, and implemented promptly.

If a member does not take the initiative to make such a withdrawal, but merely ceases to attend, then, after three absences, someone in the group should undertake to discuss the matter with the person concerned, stressing the importance of an intentional withdrawal by vocation rather than default. If the decision to withdraw from the group is not reached at this first consultation, and if that person has not resumed regular attendance after a further three weeks, there should be a final contact, and withdrawal from the group should be made official.

In practice, however, when covenant groups are properly initiated and fostered within the life of the local church, very few members withdraw.

5. Length of the Pilot Process

For the pilot group to explore the concept of covenant discipleship in depth, it is advisable to allow it to meet **for at least a year**. This may seem an unduly long time—and if a congregation is ready to participate more fully after a shorter period, then certainly the groups should be opened to all the members without delay.

But there are several factors which are conducive to a longer rather than a shorter pilot process:

The commitment to Covenant Discipleship Groups is open-ended.

If there is a distinguishing characteristic of C.D. Groups, this is it. Those who join are informed directly at the outset that their commitment is for the remainder of their Christian life. After all, when Jesus called the disciples, he did not ask them to "give it a try," or to "see if they liked it."

Commitment to C.D Groups, therefore, is not a preference, but a calling—and the pilot group needs time to confirm this in their weekly meetings so that they can affirm it for the congregation.

Of course, an open-ended commitment to Covenant Discipleship does not imply lifetime membership in the same group. This will rarely be possible, given the nature of our mobile society. People move jobs and homes, and schedules frequently change. But the commitment does mean a changed pattern of Christian discipleship; and by definition, this is a permanent change, for now and for eternity.

Questions and objections are best handled during the pilot process.

The most common objections are dealt with in Chapter Ten, and they occur with marked regularity. Ample time must be allowed during the pilot process for them to be widely aired in the congregation.

If the groups are opened to the congregation too soon, these objections will surface when there is less opportunity to deal with them effectively.

The invitation to the congregation must be carefully planned and implemented.

The extension of the groups to the congregation as a whole is in many ways a "birthing" of covenant discipleship—a critical transition, when many members will make the deeper faith commitment toward which they have been growing for some time.

This Covenant Weekend, described in Chapter Nine, must therefore be carefully planned, with ample advance notice and thorough preparation for the nurture of the groups which are formed.

When all is said and done, however, the length of the pilot process will depend on the pastoral sensitivity of the minister and the pilot members. As with all births, the time to open the groups to the congregation will be clearly recognizable—though to some extent unpredictable. The pilot group(s) should thus be watchful and ready for the culmination of their work.

Chapter Seven

The Group Meeting

When the group has drawn up and signed its covenant, it is ready for regular weekly meetings. As long as the covenant remains the point of accountability, there are no hard and fast rules for the conduct of a meeting. The following guidelines merely offer a framework within which a degree of flexibility can be exercised.

1. Time and Place

A regular meeting time should be agreed, and then made a priority for all members. Once it is perceived that the covenant is the bedrock of a person's discipleship, there are few other commitments which cannot be rearranged accordingly. Meetings should begin punctually, whether or not everyone has arrived, and should end promptly after one hour. Groups can meet at churches, in homes, in offices, at plants, in the open air. It should be kept in mind as the place is selected, however, that a degree of intimacy is desirable. Large rooms should be avoided, for example, as should places where interruptions are likely. Group members should feel completely at ease during the whole of the hour, and in an atmosphere of confidentiality.

If a regular meeting place is not possible, or if members prefer to take turns in offering hospitality for the group, then it should be clearly stated at the conclusion of each meeting where the next one will take place. Any absent members should be notified as soon as possible.

2. The Leader

It is helpful to have a leader appointed for the group during the first few weeks of its life, and this may be the pastor. But once the form of the meetings has become familiar to all of the members, leadership should rotate, the leader for the next meeting being agreed a week in advance.

The role of the leader, while different from that of the early Methodist class leader, is nonetheless important, and if any member is diffident about accepting a turn, the point should not be pressed. At the same time, hesitant members should be encouraged to assume the responsibility, and should be given every support when they accept it. More will be said about this in Chapter Eight.

71

3. The Form of the Meeting

Opening the Meeting

Covenant group meetings should always be opened with prayer, either by the leader or another member. This should be quite short, and can be followed by a joint reading aloud of the covenant. Some groups find this helpful, others do not; but it is important to proceed expeditiously to the covenant itself.

The Covenant

Each clause of the covenant is taken in order as a point of accountability. Beginning with herself or himself, the leader asks each member in turn whether the intent expressed in the clause has been fulfilled during the past week. If so, were there are any noteworthy happenings or experiences in this regard? And if not, were there any special difficulties which were encountered? Only when each member has answered does the leader proceed to the next clause.

The questions are asked without any implied judgment, but rather as a means of sharing a joint pilgrimage, and of "watching over one another in love." At the same time, the clauses are there in the covenant, and an account has to be given of the extent to which their intent has been fulfilled.

As far as possible, the entire covenant should be covered each week. But as groups develop their own dynamic, and as people begin to talk about their spiritual pilgrimages more openly, it may not be possible to cover all of the clauses in the time available. The leader should therefore exercise discretion as to which clauses will be selected for the meeting in hand, and the group should be ready to be accountable the following week for any clauses which have been omitted. The leader may also combine several clauses into one round of catechesis—for example, taking prayer and Bible study together, or worship, sacrament, and temperance.

Closing the Meeting

Meetings should be closed with prayer, and this can often take the form of an open intercession, individual concerns being shared with the group and then presented to God with full agreement.

Some groups wish to fulfill their covenant clause concerning the sacrament by asking the minister of the church to join them each week and administer Holy Communion in the closing minutes of their meeting. This is especially meaningful where several groups have agreed to meet at the same time and in the same location. Having gone through their covenants in their respective meeting places, they convene in one room for this closing act of worship.

Before the concluding prayer or sacrament, the members should make themselves accountable for any particulars of "open" clauses.

Following the conclusion of the meeting they should not forget to transact their "housekeeping" business: who is to act as leader at the next meeting, where the meeting will be held, and who will contact any absent members.

4. The Group Dynamic

By now it will be clear that the distinctive dynamic of Covenant Discipleship Groups is the dialogue between the leader and each member of the group. The accompanying diagram shows how different this is from other types of group discussion, and how important the role of the leader is in maintaining its flow. This is at once the reason for having the leadership rotate and for having it assigned to one person for the first few weeks or months, preferably someone who has already been in a covenant group, or the minister, or a staff person who has some appreciation of group dynamics.

The skill to be exercised in this catechesis is primarily that of "feedback." At times, a group member will need to be encouraged to reply to a catechetical question with more than a yes or no. On the other hand, a member may need to be discouraged from dominating the conversation with extended accounts of personal experiences. The extent to which this is handled tactfully but firmly will depend largely on the signals given by the leader in response to each response from the other members. It is the leader who must gauge the passing of time, and move through the covenant at an appropriate pace. It is likewise the leader who must sense when to take time with a member if an extended conversation proves of value to the whole group.

In short, the leader of a Covenant Discipleship Group must be no less skilled in this form of catechesis than were the early Methodist class leaders in their day. The difference is that, as far as possible, *all* group members are encouraged to develop these skills.

Flow of conversation in a typical small group

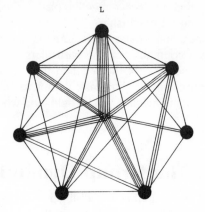

All of the members may interact, with the leader
playing a non-directive role.

Flow of conversation in a Covenant Discipleship Group

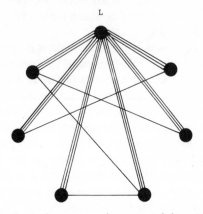

The catechetical process of accountability gives the
leader a directive role.

5. An Excerpt from a Covenant Group Meeting

Perhaps the best way to illustrate the way in which feedback can determine the flow of a meeting is to present a hypothetical covenant group meeting. As with all such "textbook" examples, the conversation will be somewhat stereotyped; but it will be drawn from actual exchanges in a number of group meetings. It will not be necessary to construct the whole of a meeting; one or two clauses will suffice. The example will include how to begin and end a meeting, and how to ensure that all items of business are properly conducted.

There are six members in this group, including the leader. If a pilot group is uncertain at first how to conduct a meeting, they may wish to begin by role-playing this dialogue; in which case it will help if the parts can be given names, rather than "First member," "Second member," etc. It should be noted in this regard that the third member should be played by a man, and the fourth member by a woman. The remaining parts can be played by a man or a woman.

Leader: Let us begin with prayer. Most gracious God, we are grateful once again to be in fellowship with each other, and to meet in the name of Jesus Christ. We have journeyed for another week as your disciples, and we come now to give an account, to you and to one another, for the steps we have taken along the way. Be with us, we pray, in the power of your Holy Spirit. Give us fresh insight into our opportunities for service; give us humility to accept our shortcomings; give us grace to love and care for one another. For we pray in the name of Jesus Christ, Amen.

Let us now recite our covenant together. *(Here would follow the covenant of the group in full.)*

We shall begin this week with the clause on prayer. We missed it last week because of our discussion on how to be more intentional in our service to those in need; but we cannot afford to lose any ground in the progress we have been making here.

Let me begin with myself. Last week I could have reported much more positively than I can this week—possibly because we didn't make ourselves accountable for this question last time. Morning prayer remains my strong point; family prayer remains weak. I find myself able to start the day with a short prayer, which I pray as soon as I get up. Then I set aside a time during the morning for more concentrated praying, along with my daily Bible reading. But at night, when we have agreed to hold our family prayers, things seem to get away from me. The day never comes to a close: it tends to "fizzle out." I have to report that I prayed on my own every day last week, but had family prayers only once.

(To first member): And how about you? Were you faithful in your prayers this week?

First member: No, I'm afraid I wasn't either. Though my difficulty is exactly the opposite to yours. I am in a firm routine now of spending the closing minutes of the day in devotional reading and prayer. The trouble is that in the morning, I am hardly able to stagger out of bed, still less think about praying. *(General group laughter).*

Leader (joining in the laughter): I know the feeling.

First member: By the time I am awake, I am caught up in the morning rush, and there seems to be no time to do anything except catch the bus. I've tried to set a time aside later in the morning, but it's difficult where I work. There are twenty other people in the room. So I really have made the evening my priority.

Leader: That's good. It's important to have a time of serious prayer when there are no other distractions. But don't think that being half asleep need prevent you from beginning the day with prayer. Just a short prayer—maybe one you can remember from Sunday school—helps enormously. The hymnal has quite a number of collects which can be learned by heart, too, and they really mean something when you say them. I sometimes think that we Protestants have reacted too strongly against this sort of prayer—we don't think we've prayed unless we have thought it up all by ourselves. Why not try learning some short prayers?

(To second member): Have you been regular in your daily prayers this week?

Second member: Oh, yes. This is something I've done for years, ever since I was a young Christian. I find that the prayers I pray at the beginning of a day are so often answered during the day that I would never think of starting out any other way. During this past week, I also made time to pause for prayer at the middle of the day, and during the afternoon as well. I find that God reaches me in all sorts of places and at all sorts of times, so I just have to be ready to respond. Though the best times I have are always in the evening, when I can go through my prayer book and pray for all the people I have on my lists. I find that a lot of people ask me to pray for them, and it helps to have everyone listed so that I don't forget anyone.

Leader: That's fine. But I wonder whether you might ask one or two of your friends to join you in a time of prayer each day? You seem to have a large number of them on your prayer list, and it may be that they would appreciate sharing in your prayers directly. It might also help you to guide your own prayer life.

(To third member): Tell us about your prayers this week.

Third member: Not much to tell, I'm afraid.

Leader: Did you have any special difficulty or problem with this?

Third member: Not really.

Leader: Just something you have to keep working at.

Third member: That's right.

Leader (to fourth member): How about your prayer life this week?

Fourth member: Yes and no.

Leader: Oh? *(General group laughter).*

Fourth member (laughing): Well, what I mean is that I did pray each day, but I wasn't really satisfied with it.

Leader: In what way?

Fourth member: I didn't feel it was quality prayer. It seemed to wander, and I never felt I was in a proper attitude of prayer. Some of the time I tried hard to get through to God, but other times I just got bored and gave up—even when I prayed with my family, I found myself thinking of other things.

Leader: But you did at least *begin* to pray.

Fourth member: Yes, I tried.

Leader: Then you fulfilled your covenant in this clause—the first person so far this week!

Fourth member: What do you mean?

Leader: Our covenant states that we will pray each day, privately and with family or friends, and that we will trust in the grace of Christ to give us strength to be obedient. This means that you were faithful to your covenant, because you waited on God in prayer. Whether or not our prayers make us *feel* prayerful is not the point. That comes by grace anyway, and is no credit to us. Our part is to be open to God's grace, to trust that the Holy Spirit is at work, regardless of how we might feel on any given day. Don't think your time was wasted. You prayed.

(To fifth member): Were you faithful in prayer this week?

Fifth member: Almost—on all but two days. I've been using the prayer diary that we looked at several weeks ago, by John Baillie.[22] And that has really helped me. Not only with beginning and ending each day in prayer, but also with names of people I should pray for, and other special concerns. It helps me realize that if we expect our prayers to be answered for our relatives and friends, then we should also pray for the problems of the world. *(To third member)* I think you would find this helpful, because it gives you a blank page each day for your own lists, and also gives you all these other prayers and ideas.

Third member: Thank you, I'll see if I can get hold of a copy. Of course, when I draw up my lists, I need to change them quite a lot, so I think I might run out of space if there was only one page each day; but at least I can get hold of a copy and see if . . .

Leader (interjecting): That's fine. Perhaps we all need to do that. But we have some other clauses in the covenant to get through. Why don't we turn to the clause on heeding the warnings of the Spirit not to sin against God and our neighbor? This clause has always seemed to have hidden ammunition for me, because every time I get ready for this meeting, I find that the Spirit has given me another new insight into my sin against people I have never met. It really came home to me this morning as I was eating breakfast. The choice was all mine, and it was all what *not* to eat. Then I thought of the millions of human beings, my brothers and sisters, whose thought this morning was very different. Their thought was not what they should not eat, but whether they would eat at all before the day was over.

Then it hit me. I was sinning—by eating while they starve. I would like us to think on this, and perhaps agree to do something more specific about it than we are right now. It has become a very pointed sin for me, and I find myself more than ever needing Christ's forgiveness.

(To first member): What warnings has the Holy Spirit given you this week concerning your sin?

First member: No doubt at all—it is my impatience. It seems that no sooner do I get to work in the mornings, than some idiot dumps a whole day's rubbish on my desk, and expects me to sort it out. I try to count to ten, and sometimes I make it. But this past week, my fuse must have been too short, because I really let three people have it in turn. I know what I'm doing when I do it, and I know I shouldn't, and I know that the Spirit is warning me every step of the way not to. But I go ahead and do it anyway.

Leader: This really seems to be a problem for you. I think you must have shared a similar story at least half-a-dozen times in the past three months. In some ways it's a matter of waiting on God's grace to help you overcome it. At least you are aware of it, and I don't doubt that anyone's patience would be tried by some of the people at your office. But as long as you are being warned that this is wrong, then you must work to overcome it.

I wonder whether it might not be something to do with your early morning stupor? If you stagger from bed to bathroom to office, I imagine that you're more than ready to lash out at anyone who calls you into the land of the living! Why not think about getting up an hour earlier in the morning? You could improve your morning prayers, and you would arrive at work much more awake. And if your evenings are well planned already, perhaps it would not take much to adjust your sleeping pattern.

First member: Oh, I don't know about that. I've tried everything to get going more quickly in the mornings.

Leader: It's just a suggestion. *(To second member):* And where have you been made more aware of your sin this week?

Second member: I'm afraid I have to confess that it has been my pride.

Leader: Can you say a little more?

Second member: I'd rather not—at least, not yet.

Leader: That's fine. But if you feel able to share anything with us next week, please do. You have a very sensitive spirit, and you always help me with your insights when we come to this clause. *(To third member)* And where did you go astray this week? *(A ripple of anticipatory laughter from the group).*

Third member: Well, as everyone might expect, I really blew it again this week! *(More laughter).*

First member: Of course.

Fifth member: What else?

Leader: The point is that now is the time of accountability. Tell us more!

Third member: Well, I know the clause states that we have to look for
the warnings of the Holy Spirit, so that we can avoid consciously sinning
against God and our neighbor. But you all know that that sounds too
heavy for me. I find that when I make a mistake, it just hits me what a
dumb thing it was to do.

So, at work last week, we had a bit of an uproar. I was working on the
sixth floor of that new building downtown, and I could hear the argument through the open windows even where I was. Come to find it was
some Vietnamese down on the ground floor wanting to get the contract
for cleaning the building. Seems they were offering a good price, but the
contract was going to be awarded to the company that does all the other
buildings. Now I knew that these Vietnamese do a good job — I've put in
carpets where they do the cleaning, and they're still like new two years
later. I *could* have gone down to put in a word for them. But I figured it
was six floors down, and what good would it do? It hit me that night. I
should have gone down. I should have said something. They were not
getting a fair shake. I blew it.

Leader (after a short silence): Thank you for that. *(To fourth member)*
In what ways were you made aware of your sin this week?

Fourth member: I've had a really bad week this week. It's my mother.
She keeps saying that I've not been a good daughter to her all these
years; but that's not true. I know that I may not have done all that I
should, but I visit her every day, I do her washing, I take her to the
doctor, I get all her prescriptions; and really, my own family life comes
second because of it. Yet once again last week she accused me of being
unfeeling towards her. I don't know whether to ask forgiveness for that
or not. Deep down, I don't *think* I am neglecting her, but every time she
says this I have doubts all over again.

Leader: This really seems to have upset you, doesn't it? Tell you what
we might do. We have the rest of the covenant to get through right now,
but perhaps one or two of us could stay behind after the meeting, and
hear a little more about it from you? Would anyone have time to stay
afterwards for a while? *(Fourth member nods, and first member indicates willingness to stay also.)* Good. Let's do that, then.

(To fifth member): And how do you give an account for this clause?

Fifth member: Actually, my experience this week is rather like yours.
It suddenly struck me last weekend how much money we are spending

in our church on new fixtures and carpets. *(To third member)* Sorry about this, 'cause I know you have the contract. But I have to say it.

Third member: That's alright. Go ahead.

Fifth member: It struck me that if we gave away even half of what we are raising for all this renovation, we could quadruple our annual giving to world hunger. Frankly, I think I should take this to the Board. I don't see any other way to be obedient now that I've received this warning from the Spirit.

Leader: Quite a warning at that! You know, it fits in with what I said a little earlier—that we ought to be doing more than we are in this area of our covenant. Maybe as a group we should present a motion to the Board next week.

Third member: I'm with you in principle, in spite of the carpets. But I don't think it'll do any good. That Board makes up its mind, and that's that.

Leader: Perhaps. But one never knows—and at least we can let them know *why* we are coming with the motion—that we're simply being obedient to the promptings of the Spirit. And if they hear the same word we are hearing, they may well do something about it. *(There is a general silence of approval.)*

Very well. We seem to be agreed. We shall need to know which of us can attend the Board meeting to make this a group presentation. We can decide that after we conclude.

(Other clauses in the covenant would then be taken in turn at the leader's discretion, following the same format of question and answer.)

Leader: That concludes the clauses in the covenant for this week. Now we come to the open clauses. I don't recall any commitments that were made last week. *(Group indicates agreement.)* Do any of us wish to make a personal covenant for next week, then?

First member: Yes, I do. I will covenant with God and make myself accountable to the group for not losing my temper at all during the coming week at the office.

Fifth member: I have one, too. I covenant with God and make myself accountable to the group for making a $50 donation this week to world hunger, and for calling each member of the Administrative Board before next week's meeting to tell them personally about our concerns.

Leader: You'll still be at the meeting on Thursday, though?

Fifth member: Oh, yes. This will be in addition.

Leader: Thank you both for those commitments. Next week the minister has agreed to attend our meeting and bring us the sacrament to conclude. To end this week, let us turn to our time of open prayer, and let us agree on our concerns before we pray.

(Members of the group offer several concerns, one of which is for the fourth member and her mother, one of which is for the Vietnamese cleaners and all immigrants who find it difficult to gain acceptance, and one of which is a prayer for guidance in presenting the concern of the group over the church renovations to the Administrative Board. These are then articulated by the leader, with the group responding: "Lord hear our prayer.")

Leader: Let us now go in peace, to serve God and our neighbor; for we are sent in Christ's name. Amen.

Before we leave, we need a leader for next week. *(First member volunteers.)* We shall meet here at the church, in this room, at the same time; and remember that the minister will join us so that we can conclude with the sacrament. Lastly, who can attend the Board meeting next Thursday to present our resolution? *(Three members indicate that they can.)* Good. Let us meet in this room at 7:00 P.M. and agree on what we shall say.

(To fourth member and first member): Now, why don't we go and get a cup of coffee somewhere, and talk about your mother. This really must be a burden for you.

Chapter Eight

Group Leadership

While the role of leader in covenant groups can only be learned in practice, there are nonetheless some guidelines which can facilitate the process. As far as possible, they were incorporated into the preceding dialogue, and are worth noting in summary.

1. Directing the Group Meeting

The leader should always keep in mind that the purpose of the group is to be accountable to a covenant. This need not make the conduct of the meeting unduly rigid, but neither should the conversation be allowed to digress into matters of general or casual interest.

The flow of dialogue should always be controlled.

The leader should encourage reticent members and discourage talkative members as and when necessary in order to allow each person to share as fully as possible in the process of accountability. At no time should the leader withdraw from the dialogue. The occasional exchange between other members should be allowed as a spontaneous component of the meeting, but the leader should resume the role of catechist as soon as possible.

The general tone of the meeting should be polite rather than intense.

There will be times when the group enters into deep sharing. This is bound to increase as the group develops its own dynamic, and need not be discouraged. It should not, however, become the objective of the meeting. The leader should ensure that more intensive sharing takes place after the group has been accountable to its covenant, and not during the hour of its meeting. The group which manages to do both at the same time has achieved a high degree of cohesiveness—something which few covenant groups attain.

Personal Problems

These will emerge from time to time during covenant group meetings, and members should not feel inhibited from raising them; nor should other members in the group regard them as an intrusion. The leader should not allow this to distract the group from the covenant, however, and should direct the meeting toward completing the task in hand before spending some further time with the member in question. Not only does this permit a freer sharing of the problem; it also prevents the group from getting into counseling which its members are not qualified to handle. An informal session with individual members after the meeting further provides an opportunity to assess whether personal problems need referral to the minister.

Advice, Encouragement, and Reproof

The role of leader in covenant groups inevitably places the onus of appropriate feedback on the person who occupies that position at any given meeting. The commitment to a mutual accountability, however, and the fact that the role of leader rotates, makes it much easier to address each member with appropriate words of guidance, praise, or correction. The more this is done by whoever is the leader each time, the more honest the group becomes in its accountability.

2. Keeping the Group Accountable

It is often the task of the leader to bring the group to a more specific accountability when it becomes clear that the clauses of the covenant are being evaded, or at least not taken as seriously as they should be. The following examples illustrate the sorts of problems which can arise, and the appropriate leadership response:

The Works of Mercy

Doing Good

If a group reaches the point where members are repeatedly saying what they ought to be doing in service to others, but find themselves not doing it, the leader must be the person to bring the group to more concrete commitments. If need be, the catechesis can be cut short to reach some decisions right there and then.

Two things need to be mentioned in this regard. First, the covenant group is not for social action or social outreach *per se*. Churches may already have—indeed, *should* have—additional groups or programs for this purpose, with covenant groups functioning alongside as a point of accountability for the means of grace. Second, however, by virtue of the grace to which covenant group members are intentionally open, they will find themselves inexorably drawn to more social service and action. The leader must be aware of this as a normative development in the life of the group so that the promptings of the Spirit to be involved with those in need are discerned and obeyed.

Avoiding Sin

The more specific a group becomes in this area, the more careful the leader will need to be in spiritual discernment. There are sins which can properly be a matter for group concern and mutual accountability; but there are more personal matters which may require professional help—problems with drugs, for example, as well as emotional disorders.

It is at this point that the "politeness" of the covenant catechesis is so important, because it permits the groups to function at a level which is within the capabilities of its members. It remains a "watching over one another in love," with a concern which ensures that members with serious problems can be guided to seek appropriate help.

The Works of Piety

Worship

If regular attendance at worship becomes a problem for anyone in the group, then members can be paired to hold each other accountable for this means of grace.

Sacrament

Likewise, if members are not availing themselves of this means of grace, the leader should take steps to have the group receive the sacrament. Preferably, members should receive it at least once a week.

Prayer

If members consistently report that they are not maintaining their covenant of prayer, the leader should suggest a more specific approach: the keeping of a prayer diary, the learning of special prayers, the intentional grouping of members for corporate prayer, a special study of the classical disciplines of prayer, etc.

Scripture

By the same token, if daily Bible reading proves to be a problem for the group, the leader should suggest a specific course of study, either with the use of a commentary, or with a daily devotional guide. If necessary, accountability for reading certain verses can be allocated to each member.

Fellowship

The weekly covenant group meeting can be regarded as the fulfillment of this clause of the covenant. The leader should ensure, however, that each member is regarding it as a serious point of accountability, and not merely a fellowship meeting.

Fasting

The problem with this means of grace is that, in our present culture, fasting is often regarded as a dieting fad. This is why it is helpful at first to include it in the covenant as a general resolve to care for one's body through temperance in all things. As the group develops its disciplines, members may wish to adopt fasting as a spiritual exercise, and can amend the clause accordingly.

3. Leadership of the Group

When it is remembered that the "leader" referred to throughout the preceding pages can be any member of the group at any given time, the principle of mutual accountability emerges with even greater force and clarity. An important difference between Covenant Discipleship Groups and the early Methodist class meeting is that those of us in the twentieth century have been given many more gifts and talents to use for the coming of God's New Age than our eighteenth century forebears could ever have imagined. And among these gifts are the advantages of better education, and the cumulative effects of a free society, giving each of us a capacity for mutual interaction.

Allowing Leadership to Emerge

This does not mean, however, that certain group members will not emerge with leadership qualities particularly suited to Covenant Discipleship Groups. Qualities of spiritual discernment, human sensitivity, organizational ability, and pastoral concern are bound to surface in the weekly meetings; and where this is the case, such persons should be encouraged to develop their leadership potential.

Contact Persons

A good way of allowing this to happen, once the groups have been introduced to the congregation a a whole, is to ask each group to appoint one of its members as a liaison with the minister for the purposes of pastoral oversight and administration. To have one person so designated makes for easier communication with all of the members, and affords the minister an opportunity for monitoring the progress of each group in particular.

By identifying such members as liaison, or contact persons, the role of leader continues to be shared at the weekly meetings, and a sense of mutual collegiality is maintained. But this also allows leadership to emerge naturally where it is present—as, for example, where the liaison or contact person for a group is also a regular leader at the weekly meetings.

Indeed there are some groups where this will be necessary if they are not to flounder during their formative months.

Spiritual "Muscle"

This is not a recommendation for the formal relationship which Wesley and his preachers had with the early class leaders; but it is to suggest that something very similar may develop quite spontaneously in some churches. As with other aspects of congregational life, this will be a gift of the Spirit, to be accepted graciously, or squandered thoughtlessly. Careful pastors and sensitive covenant groups will know what is happening, however, and will react accordingly. For the leadership fostered by these weekly meetings will, in fact, be the spiritual "muscle"of the church.

Chapter Nine

Opening Groups to the Congregation

When the pilot group has been meeting for several months, it is time to invite the whole congregation to take part. It must be remembered that only a minority of the membership will respond to this invitation, but it is extremely important to *extend* it to everyone. Not only does this ensure that the call is made as full as possible; it also precludes any feeling among the membership that the groups have deliberately been made exclusive.

1. The Covenant Group Weekend

The best way to make this invitation is by announcing in advance that, on a particular weekend, covenant groups are going to be introduced into the life and work of the whole church. This should obviously be well-advertised, and invitations to attend should be extended as far as possible on a personal basis, working through individuals and through official church bodies.

Friday: Informal Testimony

On the Friday evening, it is a good idea to begin with a church-wide meeting—if practicable, a covered dished supper—at which the minister or a guest speaker can describe the groups in some detail, and at which members of the pilot group can talk about their participation in the covenant thus far. It is also a good time for questions to be aired, especially those which indicate any lingering doubts or objections to the groups. To have discussed these thoroughly in the pilot group proves to be extremely helpful in reassuring people that the whole concept is vocational, and will not be imposed on everyone in the church.

Saturday: Training Workshops

On the Saturday, preferably in the morning and the afternoon, two training workshops can be held. In the first, the theology behind the groups can be explained, along with something of their origin in the Methodist heritage; and in the second, it can be explained how a group functions, perhaps with members of the pilot group performing a short role play. In this way it can be shown how the catechetical form of the meeting is not at all threatening, but is rather an assurance of comradeship on a common journey. The role plays can also provide a convincing demonstration of the value of mutual accountability. When other persons are invited to join the pilot group members in such an exercise, there is almost always an immediate spontaneity—an outpouring of concern for discipleship and a need to be in company with those of like mind and spirit. It is the discovery, albeit in a training context, that the Christian journey is not solitary—that there are indeed companions along the way.

Sunday: Invitation to Commitment

On the Sunday morning, the weekend comes sharply into focus with the worship service, at which the invitation is made to the whole congregation to join a covenant group. Several points need to be kept in mind in preparation for this:

The Order of Worship

This should indicate clearly that the focus of the worship service is to invite persons to enter into a new form of mutual accountability for their discipleship. The hymns should be selected with an emphasis on service and obedience to the will of God, and the text for the sermon should focus on the theme of working out our salvation—Matthew 21:28-32, for example, or Philippians 2:12-13.

The Bulletin

There should be a clear indication in the order of worship that there will be an invitation following the sermon to make a public commitment to group membership. The bulletin should include an insert on which there is printed a sample covenant, such as that on page 64. Before the invitation is made, the minister should refer to this, so that people are aware of the commitment they are being asked to make. The insert should make clear that this is only a sample, and should include at the foot of the page a place for each person to sign her or his name, indicating a response to the invitation.

The Invitation

This should be done without any pressure or manipulation, and should take the form of a call to the front of the sanctuary to join with the minister(s) in an open prayer. A suitable prayer for this purpose is the dedication from Wesley's *Covenant Service:*

> *I am no longer my own, but thine.*
> *Put me to what thou wilt, rank me with thom thou wilt;*
> *put me to doing, put me to suffering;*
> *let me be employed for thee or laid aside for thee,*
> *exalted for thee or brought low for thee;*
> *let me be full, let me be empty;*
> *let me have all things, let me have nothing;*
> *I freely and heartily yield all things to thy pleasure and disposal.*
> *And now, O glorious and blessed God, Father, Son and Holy Spirit,*
> *thou art mine, and I am thine.*
> *So be it.*
> *And the covenant which I have made on earth,*
> *let it be ratified in heaven.*
> *Amen.*

Those who respond should be asked to sign the bulletin insert, and bring it to the front of the church when they come forward to offer their prayer of commitment with the minister. The signed inserts then remain as a record of everyone who came forward.

Two Further Words about the Invitation

It may be that there are some members in the congregation who are diffident about coming forward during a worship service for any reason.

It should therefore be announced at the end of the service that signed bulletin inserts can be left with an usher, or later at the church office. In this way, the invitation is made fully inclusive, and people who were absent from the service for any reason have an opportunity to respond.

There should also be a word of explanation about the invitation at the conclusion of the Saturday workshops. Those who have attended these training sessions are most likely to be the ones who form the nucleus of the groups, and they should be asked to take the initiative in coming forward at the worship service the following day. Their movement from the body of the congregation will encourage others to come forward, and their act of public commitment will be an important witness for themselves and the whole of the church.

After the Covenant Prayer

The people should then be asked to return to their seats, and an announcement made about a follow-up meeting to be held later that day, or on an evening during the following week. If it is held on the Sunday, everyone should be encouraged to attend, including any who did not come forward during the service. If it is held later in the week, then each person who came forward should be contacted personally and asked to attend. It should be made clear in the announcement that the purpose of the follow-up meeting is to form the groups and launch them into their regular weekly meetings.

It cannot be stated too strongly that once the invitation has been made on a church-wide basis, the groups should be organized that very week and encouraged to start their meetings as soon as possible.

2. Organizing the Groups

Because of the nature and dynamic of Covenant Discipleship Groups, personal preferences in membership matter less than in other types of small group. Even so, it is helpful to avoid any conflicts of personality if at all possible, and the following method of initiating the groups has been found to work easily and effectively.

The Follow-Up Meeting

The follow-up meeting should be held in a large room, with sheets of newsprint at various places around the walls. After some introductory remarks, during which the purpose of the groups can be re-stated and any further questions addressed, the minister should ask for some days and times which might be convenient for group meetings. As these are suggested from the floor, they should be written up on separate sheets of newsprint, until all possible times and days are prominently on display. More pieces of newsprint should be added if need be.

Everyone in the room should then be asked to sign the sheet which indicates the most convenient time for them. This permits a great degree of movement and flexibility, during the course of which people can select not only the best day and time, but also their preferred companions, without giving the appearance of rejecting anyone or any group.

The Role of the Pilot Group

The process also allows members of the pilot group to disperse themselves among the groups, so that no group is without someone who can act as leader for the first few weeks. The Saturday workshops will have provided further leadership resources, but should there be a group without anyone who can act in this capacity, the minister will have to assign such a person. A group without leadership in the initial stages will quickly lose its sense of purpose and commitment.

It may be that members of the pilot group(s) express a strong preference to remain together as a group, rather than disperse among the new groups. If this is the case, then a solution which has proved readily acceptable is to ask the pilot members to give "double time" for several months—i.e., to continue to meet as a group, but, in addition, to meet with new groups until they have grasped the basics of covenant discipleship. Most pilot groups who wish to stay together are more than willing to contribute the extra time.

3. Group Membership

During this organizing procedure, a number of questions may be raised about the constituency of the groups, and the following guidelines should be noted.

No Restrictions

Covenant groups function without any membership restrictions concerning age, sex, or marital status. For contextual reasons, a group might be made up of men or women only, but the great majority are mixed, since the mutual accountability of discipleship applies to all persons alike. Some married couples, for example, prefer to join the same group; others prefer to be in separate groups. Some families wish to be in a group together; in other instances, children prefer to be in covenant apart from their parents. There are no hard and fast rules in this regard.

Groups for Young People

It will be clear from the catechetical process of the groups that the format permits participation by young people at a much earlier age than would be the case if faith sharing were the agenda. The purpose being accountability, however, there is an opportunity to form groups of young people from the age of 11-12 upwards as an important part of the nurturing programs of the church.

The writing of the covenant for such groups has to be undertaken carefully, and the leadership has to be provided by older persons—especially in dealing with the questions of practical discipleship as opposed to those concerned with the means of grace. At the same time, the capacity for mutual accountability and leadership among young people should not be underestimated. A young persons' covenant group may be ready for self-supervision more quickly than is expected.

Intergenerational Groups

Reference has already been made to the fact that some families will prefer to be in a group together, and others will wish to divide. A word should therefore be mentioned about the value of having groups consisting of adults and young people together.

For a young person to take part in a catechetical process in which adults are being held accountable for their Christian discipleship is a profoundly formative experience. Indeed, the perceived lack of such accountability among adults is a significant factor in the loss of many young people from the ranks of committed discipleship in the contemporary church. If a young person wishes to be part of a covenant group with her or his peers, this should in no way be discouraged. On the other hand, a young person should not be discouraged from wishing to be part of a group with adults.

Older persons do not need to feel embarrassed or diffident about being accountable to a young person. Nothing could be more salutary for both.

Recruitment of New Members

Once a group is formed and is meeting regularly, it should be part of its task to invite new members to join. For this purpose, it is best if new groups are limited to four or five members at first, to allow for some expansion before having to subdivide into two groups of four.

The only rule for receiving new members is that they understand first of all the nature of the covenant commitment, and that they be willing to sign the particular covenant the group is using. There are opportunities for changing the covenant in due course, but not as the occasion of welcoming a new member.

This is not to deny the new person a part in the group, but rather to stress the nature of the accountability to which he or she is being called. The opportunity to share in subsequent revisions of the covenant will follow.

Trial Visitation

A prospective new member should be asked to attend the group for three sessions before making the decision to join. By the same token, visitors should be allowed to attend only three times before being asked to decide whether or not to join. The format of the group meetings is such that visits of this nature can be readily assimilated; but the nature of the group commitment makes it necessary to limit the participation of those who remain undecided.

Visitors or prospective members should be given the option of whether to take part in the catechetical process, or to observe—a further reason for limiting their visits to three.

Chapter Ten

Dealing with Objections

As the groups are introduced to a congregation, there will be misgivings, if not outright criticism. Objections usually come under six broad categories, to each of which there are appropriate responses.

1. Covenant groups imply an elitism.

Objection

There are those who feel that when people gather into small groups for any form of spiritual activity, there is a distinction implied between them and everyone else in the church. And the only inference to draw from such a distinction, it is argued, is that such persons regard themselves as superior.

Answer

The answer to this is that members of covenant groups, far from implying a spiritual superiority, confess to each other, and to the body of the church, that they are unable to maintain their discipleship on their own. They need the help and support of others, *even to keep the essentials of their faith!* If this is a superiority, it is a superiority of need.

As we noted in Part One, the closest parallels to covenant groups in contemporary society are organizations such as Alcoholics Anonymous or Weight Watchers, where a common weakness is confessed and dealt with through the help of others who have the same problem. Members of covenant groups likewise confess a common weakness: their inability to be obedient disciples of Jesus Christ. Even though they are restored to communion with God in Christ, there remains what the Wesleys described as "inbred sin"—that residual old nature which still resists the gracious initiatives of God. The mark of covenant group members is their recognition of this weakness, and the taking of some elementary steps to deal with it. They have seen the importance of watching over one another in love, and their sense of need is far removed from any feeling of superiority.

2. Discipleship is a personal matter between the believer and God.

Objection

There are those who are reluctant to render themselves accountable to others on the grounds that their relationship with God is personal and private, and likewise their discipleship. Obedience to God is an individual matter, and, they argue, there can be no accounting for it to anyone but God.

Answer

The answer to this objection must begin with the fact that it represents one of the most pervasive ailments of the Western church, with a pedigree stretching far back into the theological and cultural history of the last three centuries. Would that discipleship were just a personal matter—but it is not. The Christian life is one of accountability to God *and* to one's neighbor; and just as sin is both personal and social, so is the call to discipleship. To be accountable to one another for Christian obedience is to make a commitment that ceases to be optional. Private discipleship, on the other hand, can always choose the easy way out.

Besides which, covenant groups do not insist on personal confession. The catechetical form of the meetings makes it possible for members to be accountable without divulging anything they do not wish to share with the group. On most occasions, of course, sharing does take place in order that each person can be supportive of the others. But covenant groups can and frequently do function without an intensive experience. Their purpose is accountability.

3. Affirming a written covenant is unnecessarily legalistic.

Objection

There are those who object to covenant groups on the grounds that they restrict the freedom of discipleship which is the mark of the new life in Christ, and tie a person to unnecessary rules and regulations.

Answer

This, too, of course, has a long history in the Western church, and is reinforced today by a consumerist culture which has taught us to demand what we choose, and reject what displeases us. It is further reinforced by the deceptive emphasis on personal freedom which a technological society uses to ease the frustrations of homogenized living. For the Christian, however, such personal freedoms are not only illusory, but dangerous, in that they disparage obedient discipleship and underestimate the ingenuity of human sin.

The fact of the matter is that Christians throughout the history of the church have found the means of grace to be altogether trustworthy. Compared with the unreliability and volatility of the individual Christian commitment and experience, these seasoned habits are foolproof. And just as people willingly bind themselves to contracts which they wish to keep inviolate in the midst of their own inconsistencies, so Christians need to bind themselves willingly to those means of grace which empower their works of obedience, and thereby maintain their relationship with God in Christ.

One need only note how readily persons sign financial and real estate agreements, often committing decades of their lives to repayments, to make the obvious contrast with Christians who are unwilling to make even a minimal commitment to what are self-evidently the basics of their discipleship.

4. A fear of "virtuoso religiousness"

Objection

The fourth category of objection is perhaps the most understandable: a feeling of inferiority on the part of those who perceive themselves as quite ordinary Christians, and therefore bound to be "shown up" by the more "saintly" persons who belong to covenant groups. By no means least of the threatening figures in this regard is the minister, who is regarded—usually for no good reason—as the one most practiced in spiritual discipline.

Answer

One of the most rewarding aspects of introducing the groups into the life of a church is to encounter the tremendous relief which is expressed when these "ordinary" Christians find at the very first meeting that the "saints" are just as ordinary as themselves.

This is especially the case when the minister of the church takes part in the catechetical process, and has to admit to a neglect of what are some of the essentials of discipleship. To find, for example, that one's minister has difficulty in maintaining a daily prayer schedule, or devotional Bible study, is a heartening discovery for the average church member. Not that this in any way reduces the pastoral standing of the minister. On the contrary, by identifying him or her as a fellow pilgrim in the Christian life, it provides encouragement for those who lack confidence in their faith and discipleship.

By the same token, those who are regarded as saints in the congregation are seen in a new light. Intensity of Christian experience does not count in covenant groups, nor does fervency of prayer. What is on record here week by week is an accountability to discipleship, *regardless of experience or intensity of faith*. Those whose discipleship has been tempered through years of trial and error in the path of obedience thus emerge with true authority; and those whose "experience" has perhaps tended to obscure a brittle and uncertain Christian life are brought back to the essentials of the faith.

5. *Covenant Groups deny the freedom of the Holy Spirit.*

Objection

It is not without some degree of irony that this category of objection should often come from persons who proclaim and live out a fine Christian discipleship in the power of the Holy Spirit. Not least does it come from those who have received the baptism of the Spirit in what Wesley termed the *second blessing.* The objections stem from the strong conviction that the whole of Christian discipleship is an expression of the Holy Spirit, a free gift of God. Any effort on our part to engineer such grace, or any implication that our own efforts are necessary to maintain it, is therefore tantamount to a denial of the gifts of the Spirit. Indeed, to place such an emphasis on our obligations of discipleship prevents us from expecting the power of the Holy Spirit; and what we do not expect, we do not receive.

Answer

The answer to such an objection is twofold. In the first place, covenant groups do not deny the freedom of the Holy Spirit. Rather, they acknowledge the variety of God's spiritual gifts. Those whose particular gift is the spiritual power to maintain the obedience of their discipleship without a point of mutual accountability clearly have no need of a covenant group. That does not, however, deny the validity of the groups for those who lack such spiritual power.

Second, it must be asked whether participation in a covenant group by those who have particular spiritual gifts might not be an appropriate way of sharing them with those whose obedience comes more painstakingly. To feel so secure in the presence and power of the Holy Spirit as to disdain a weekly check-up can be the mark of a pride which borders on true humility, but which is pride nonetheless.

6. A lifetime commitment to a group is impracticable and unrealistic.

Objection

Of all objections, this is perhaps the most honest. Given the mobile nature of our society, it is argued, few if any of us are in a position any more to make this sort of commitment. Rather than make a promise which will prove impossible to keep, would it not be more realistic to enter into a conditional covenant, stipulating a limited time? If the group wishes to renew the covenant for a further period, that is always possible. Besides which, the objection continues, a person's needs will change through a lifetime, and it is unlikely that this particular form of commitment will prove consistently helpful.

Answer

This objection seems to be pragmatic, but frequently it is the final resistance of a person who is close to a deeper Christian commitment; which is what makes it disarmingly honest.

The first answer is to make clear that joining a Covenant Discipleship Group is commitment to the practice of mutual accountability, and not to one particular group. Yes, people are going to move around the country, change employment, and change churches; and yes, people will develop in their Christian discipleship. But C.D. Groups are the means of being accountable for the necessary basis of that discipleship: the works of mercy and the works of piety. They provide the anchor for those who are called to accountability. The first step to be taken on arriving at a new church, therefore, is to join a C.D. Group—or start one.

The second answer is back to the question of common sense. *If* Christ is the way, the truth, and the life, and *if* there are well-tried ways of opening ourselves to the grace of his Spirit, the issue is not whether a lifetime commitment is practicable or realistic, but whether we can afford *not* to make it. The development of Christian discipleship never outgrows the basics.

Chapter Eleven

Covenant Discipleship Groups in the Ongoing Life and Work of the Church

To invite the whole congregation to join covenant groups is at once to make them an integral part of the body of the church. Regardless, therefore, of the number of members who actually join, it is important to identify their particular contribution to the life and work of the witnessing community. They should not be a hidden or mysterious component of the church, and the opportunity to join them should be made regularly available.

The Invitation to Discipleship

There are many churches where, at the conclusion of the sermon on a Sunday morning, the invitation is extended to make a commitment to Christian discipleship. From time to time, this invitation can be adapted to one which offers the further commitment of a covenant group. This keeps the people aware of the nature of the groups, and also gives the opportunity to people who wish to deepen their discipleship.

The Covenant Book

It is a quiet but effective witness to have a special book on display in the church, perhaps on a lectern in the narthex, or at the rear of the sanctuary, in which all of the covenant group members are listed. There are attractively bound volumes available today with blank pages, in which members can sign their names, each on a separate page, along with the date of their commitment to a group. A sample covenant can be written at the beginning of the volume, along with a short explanation of why the book is on display. In this way, the whole church can see who is in a group, or "in covenant."

103

The book can also be used as a public witness when new members join, as they sign their names in the book after making their public commitment.

Quarterly Meetings

One of the moribund customs of early Methodism which offers an opportunity for the development of the covenant groups is the quarterly meeting. Once every three months, it can be a rich experience to gather all the covenant groups together for a covered dish supper and a devotional evening—in many ways the modern equivalent of the early Methodist lovefeasts. After the meal, everyone should remain at the tables for a time of open testimony from the groups: how each is faring in its pilgrimage; particular trials and triumphs; new paths of discipleship; new ways of service in the world; new insights into sin and grace; indeed, anything which needs to be shared.

This is also a good time to invite other interested church members to attend, and to share in the collective experience of the groups. A large gathering is often less threatening to those who still have reservations about what happens in the intimacy of the small gatherings, and can be a way of introducing them directly to their nature and purpose.

Covenant Sunday

If there is a day in the Methodist year which is ready-made for covenant groups, this is it. It no longers functions as it used to in early Methodism—originally it was a Watchnight Service—but it nonetheless provides an opportunity to celebrate the work of the covenant groups, and to renew their witness.

The order of worship on that day should include part, if not all, of Wesley's *Covenant Service,* which is available in *The Book of Worship.*[23] This leads the people through a review of their discipleship during the past year, and brings them to a re-commitment of their covenant for the year ahead. At the point in the service at which the *Covenant Prayer* is recited, those who are in covenant groups should be asked to come forward, so that they might face the congregation as the prayer is recited. At the same time, any new members can be asked to come forward to make a commitment.

The Renewing of Group Covenants

Prior to the service on Covenant Sunday, each group should be asked to review its covenant, and make any adjustments to the clauses which members feel are necessary. This is a helpful point of renewed accountability, because it allows group members to evaluate the past year, and to take account of any new insights they have acquired. When they are called forward for the covenant prayer, each group should present a copy of their renewed covenant to the minister as a token of continuing commitment.

"Muscle" for the Church

As we have noted, Wesley described the class meeting as the "sinews" of the early Methodist movement. Today, there is the same need for "muscle" in the church. Muscle is not the whole body: yet without it, the body is weak and ineffective. Moreover, what ought to be healthy growth can easily become excess fat, draining the pastoral resources of a congregation.

But when there is well-tuned muscle, the body is strong, lean, and active. This is what happens when Covenant Discipleship Groups provide the opportunity for groups of committed Christians to exercise accountability for their discipleship. As with all muscle which has not been used for some time, there will be aches and pains. The activity engendered by these groups will not always be convenient. But in the long term, they will equip the church for a discipleship in the world which is resilient, faithful, and challenging.

It will also be a costly discipleship; and for this, too, the church must be ready.

The Presence and Power of the Groups

Most important of all for the local church, the groups must be recognized for what they are: a means of grace for the whole body. Just as those "in covenant" come to receive the grace of Christ in new ways through their accountability for discipleship, so those churches which initiate and foster them as part of their life and work are infused with new grace. This is not to identify those in covenant as any more virtuous than their fellow church members, but merely to draw the obvious inference from our earlier study of Wesley's doctrine of grace: that when there are some who open themselves more fully to God's gracious initiatives, then grace moves more freely and efficaciously through the body as a whole.

Needless to say, the signs of this grace are not immediately self-evident; nor is this a dimension of covenant groups which can be too readily assumed. But it is a deep spiritual truth that when some members of a church heed the call to commitment and apply themselves to the imperative of mutual accountability, that church becomes spiritually more attuned to the will of God, and more healthy in all aspects of its discipleship. And in turn, it becomes more a means of grace for the community in which it is called to witness and to serve. Such, at least, was Wesley's understanding of the call to discipleship, the "Scripture Way of Salvation." [24]

Chapter Twelve

Covenant Discipleship Groups and Early Methodist Class Meetings

For those readers who have followed the adaptation of the class meeting to this model of Covenant Discipleship Groups, it may be helpful to summarize the differences and similarities between the two.

Differences

1. Covenant groups are limited to seven members, whereas class meetings were initially formed with up to twelve members, and often became larger. The reason for the smaller number in covenant groups is the limit of one hour for each meeting, during which time each member must be accountable for each clause of a covenant containing from seven to ten clauses. A larger group membership would therefore be impracticable.

This is why, when a group reaches a membership of eight, it should subdivide into two new groups of four, thereby permitting further expansion of each of the new groups. While this rule is not to be rigidly enforced in the case of a group which feels it important to stay together for a period of time, it should not be overlooked indefinitely. The purpose of the group is accountability, and this should not be displaced by a wish to engage in more informal sharing—the usual reason a group wishes to stay together rather than divide.

2. Covenant groups adopt a format of mutual accountability, whereas the class meetings were formed around a leader. The reason for this is that covenant groups are for the most part formed from members of local churches rather than from people who are unfamiliar with the Christian faith. Not only is the instruction which the early classes provided available in and through other church activities. There is also the more broadly social factor that, as a model of discipleship for

the late twentieth century, the covenant groups must take into account
the two centuries of Christian education which have passed since
Wesley's day. As we have noted, leadership in the covenant groups is an
important factor, but it is not necessary to have the sort of "sub-pastor"
role in the groups which the early class leader filled in Wesley's day.

3. Covenant groups meet for one hour, whereas class meetings
sometimes lasted for a whole evening. This again is to take account of
the fact that the covenant groups are little churches, designed to meet
within the larger church with its structured order and activity. Quite
apart from the different pace of life in the late twentieth century, many
of the fellowship needs which were met by the original class meetings
are now met in other ways, either in the church or in and through other
social networks.

The importance of the covenant groups, on the other hand, is
accountability for discipleship. This need not and should not limit other
forms of group activity, either in the church or beyond it. Bible study
groups fulfill a different function, as do sharing groups of various sorts
and purposes. Action groups, discussion groups, outreach groups, and
growth groups are likewise complementary. Indeed, it is possible to hold
a covenant group meeting for the first hour of an evening, and then
continue with another form of group activity afterwards—a Bible study
group, for example, or an outreach group.

By limiting the covenant group meetings to one hour, members can
meet together for mutual accountability without, on the one hand,
being drawn into discussions which are not part of the covenant, or on
the other hand, having personal schedules unduly disrupted. Meetings
can be scheduled at a wide range of times: early morning, mid-morning,
lunch, early evening, or even late at night. Students who meet in college
dormitories, for example, find that a covenant meeting at 10:00 P.M. to
close the day is not only more feasible for many people: it is also a good
time to be consciously accountable for what has happened during the
preceding day and week.

4. The covenant groups draw up a written agreement to which
they are accountable, whereas the early class meetings followed a
catechetical process in which the leader dwelt largely on the spiritual life
of each member. The written covenant is used primarily because the
early class meeting presupposed the adherence of each member to

the *General Rules* of the societies, which were even more detailed than the covenant clauses suggested for this model.

The covenant groups might be said to fall somewhere between the societies and the class meetings in their nature and purpose. In Wesley's day, the societies increasingly represented the ecclesial order which the Church of England failed to provide for the early Methodists, notwithstanding Wesley's exhortations to attend the local parish church. In our own time, the church is, by and large, much more sensitive to such needs, and the structure of Wesley's societies is not required in such detail. On the other hand, the need to be accountable to a disciplined Christian lifestyle is not always found in the larger church, and the written covenant ensures that the fellowship of a small group does not preclude the accountability for discipleship which it is intended to provide.

Similarities

1. Membership of covenant groups is limited, as with class meetings, to those who are willing to make a firm commitment to an agreed pattern of Christian discipleship. The covenant which the group formulates and agrees to adopt is based on the three components of Wesley's *General Rules:* avoiding sin, doing good, and availing oneself of the means of grace of the church.

2. The format of covenant group meetings is catechetical, as was that of the class meetings. One person in the group acts as a leader and asks each member in turn whether the clauses of the covenant have been kept as intended. The dynamic of the group, like the class meeting, is not one of spontaneous sharing, but of guided dialogue. The leader assesses the need for more or less response from each member, and keeps the flow of the meeting within the time allowed.

3. Weekly attendance at the meetings is required, as with the class meeting, and absences are quickly followed up with a personal contact. Since the accountability between the group members is wholly mutual, repeated absences detract from the group objectives and cannot be permitted.

4. The commitment to the group is open-ended. In contrast with many small group programs in the church today, which continue only as long as people find them helpful or fulfilling, covenant groups are for those who wish to make a lifetime commitment to the barest essentials for Christian discipleship. As with the class meetings, this is made clear at the outset. Those who became Methodists in Wesley's day regarded the class meeting as a weekly discipline for as long as they were Methodists; and this commitment was usually made for life.

5. Covenant groups are structured within the larger church, as were the class meetings, and are accountable not only to their own covenant disciplines, but also to the ordinances of the church. This larger accountability is exercised, not only in affirming the necessity of the means of grace, but also in relating at certain critical points to the wider life and work of the local congregation.

Conclusion

Two Warnings and
a Promise

The commitment made by members of Covenant Groups almost always occasions an infectious exuberance, and in the first few weeks of their meetings there are many positive experiences. The hunger for this sort of fellowship is real, and it will be accompanied by a fascination for the new and the exciting, from which none of us is altogether immune. Before they are formed and begin to meet, therefore, it is important to issue two warnings—and along with the warnings, a promise.

The "Doldrums"

The catechetical process of being accountable for aspects of discipleship which have hitherto been neglected or taken for granted gives each group a wealth of insight and challenge during the first two or three months of meeting together. After three or four months, however, a sense of routine sets in. The questions seem to become stereotyped. Answers lack spontaneity, and members begin to question the validity and usefulness of the whole exercise.

It should be quite clearly stated to new groups that this time of "doldrums" is to be anticipated, and for two reasons. The most immediate cause is the wish to turn to something new when the novelty of the groups has worn off. In part this is reflective of our culture's preoccupation with self-fulfillment, and it should be resisted. Indeed, this is one of the most important functions of the groups.

There is a deeper spiritual reason for the "doldums," however, which can best be described as getting a "second wind." Most churchgoers today are out of practice when it comes to accountable discipleship. Many have been spectators in church, watching and perhaps admiring those who seem to be committed to their faith, though not really wishing to join them in the work of Christ's New Age. But in a covenant group, there is no avoiding the challenge of discipleship. While this is exhilarating at first, there comes a time when the routine of the task begins to take hold—where the daily grind requires stamina.

When a group goes through this period of "breaking in," it should be explained that this is exactly what covenant discipleship is all about. It is an agreement to watch over one another. We are in covenant, not merely to share the high points of our journey, important though these are, but rather to sustain and support in the midst of the routine and the commonplace.

If a group remains faithful to its covenant through these "doldrums," it is not long before the rough and tumble of living in the world brings them to realize even more profoundly the value of their common bond. Such times of apparent aimlessness are no more than a test of the commitment they have made, a searching and tempering of their discipleship, a moving away from self-serving interests to those which are Christ-serving. It is a form of spiritual growth well attested in the history of the Christian faith; but groups need to know about it at the outset, and be ready for it.

Complacency

Another word of caution to new groups should be to warn against the danger of becoming complacent about their catechesis. When this happens, it usually takes the form of thoughtless answers from members who are coming to the meetings from habit rather than commitment. At times it can even take the form of patently dishonest answers, leaving the rest of the group at a serious disadvantage, and ultimately having an adverse effect on the meetings as a whole.

Groups should know in advance that this is a real danger to their purpose and commitment. Suggestions have already been made about ways in which the leader can address such problems each week with specific recommendations, but a general warning to all groups that this can undermine their very identity should be given clearly at this formative stage.

The Promise of Grace

At the same time, it is important to stress to new groups that they must expect the grace of God to invade their lives in new ways, because now they are making themselves accountable for the means through which it flows. And grace will indeed flow—very probably in ways for which they are not quite ready.

It means, for example, that as members become disciplined in daily prayer and Bible study, in worship, sacrament and fellowship, they will consciously experience the love, the power, and the justice of God as never before. Prayer will be more efficacious in their lives; guidance will be more direct; correction will be more specific; and service will be more demanding. There will be a greater awareness of the sin of the world and their participation in it; there will be a stronger call to work for the New Age of Jesus Christ and their opportunities for service will become more evident.

Being accountable for our discipleship is far from an exercise in self-improvement. It is opening ourselves to the gracious initiatives of the Holy Spirit for which we have no less than God's promise in Jesus Christ. Wesley's words still ring loud and clear, calling us to the unfinished task of discipleship:

We go on from grace to grace, while we are careful to "abstain from all appearance of evil," and are "zealous of good works," as we have opportunity, doing good to all men; while we walk in all His ordinances blameless, therein worshipping Him in spirit and in truth; while we take up our cross, and deny ourselves in every pleasure that does not lead us to God.[25]

References

1. *The Methodist Hymnal* (Nashville: United Methodist Publishing House), #92.
2. Ibid.
3. "The Nature, Design, and General Rules of the United Societies, in London, Bristol, Kingswood, Newcastle-upon-Tyne, &c." (1743), *The Works of John Wesley,* 14 vols. (London: Wesleyan Methodist Book Room, 1872. Repr. ed. Grand Rapids, Michigan: Baker Book House, 1979), 8:269.
4. Albert C. Outler, ed. *John Wesley.* Library of Protestant Thought. (New York: Oxford University Press, 1964), p. vii.
5. Frank Baker, "John Wesley's Churchmanship," *London Quarterly and Holborn Review* 185 (1960):210. See also *John Wesley and the Church of England* (Nashville: Abingdon, 1970), pp. 4-5.
6. Ibid.
7. *The Oxford Edition of the Works of John Wesley,* Editor in Chief, Frank Baker, Vol. 25: *Letters I: 1721-1739,* ed. Frank Baker (Oxford: at the Clarendon Press, 1980), pp. 615-16. See also Vol. 11: *The Appeals to Men of Reason and Religion and Certain Related Open Letters,* ed. Gerald R. Cragg (1975), p. 324.
8. "A Plain Account of the People Called Methodists," *Works,* 8:248.
9. "Reasons Against a Separation from the Church of England," *Works,* 13:226.
10. Sermon "On Schism," *Works,* 6:406ff.
11. Josiah Woodward, *An Account of the Rise and Progress of the Religious Societies in the City of London, &c.* (London, 1698). See also John S. Simon, *John Wesley and the Religious Societies* (London: Epworth Press, 1921), pp. 9-27.
12. *The Journal of the Rev. John Wesley, A.M.,* ed. Nehemiah Curnock. Standard Edition, 8 vols. (London: Epworth Press, 1909-1916), 3:33.
13. The terms "Moravian church" and "Unitas Fratrum" (Unity of the Brethren) are used interchangeably to describe the group which settled at Herrnhut—as is the term "Herrnhuter." See Gillian Lindt Gollin, *Moravians in Two Worlds: A Study of Changing Communities* (New York: Columbia University Press, 1967).

14. *Journal,* 2:496.
15. *Journal,* 1:372.
16. "The Large Minutes," *Works,* 8:322-24.
17. *Works,* 8:269-70.
18. *Works,* 8:269. See also "A Plain Account of the People Called Methodists," *Works,* 8:253.
19. *Journal,* 3:449-50, 495.
20. *Methodist Hymnal,* #152.
21. James W. Fowler, *Stages of Faith: The Psychology of Human Development and the Quest for Meaning* (San Francisco: Harper & Row, 1981).
22. John Baillie, *A Dairy of Private Prayer* (New York: Scribners, 1936). This has been reprinted many times.
23. *The Book of Worship* (Nashville: Methodist Publishing House, 1964).
24. Sermon, "The Scripture Way of Salvation," *The Standard Sermons of John Wesley,* ed. E.H. Sugden 2 vols. (London: Epworth Press, 1921), 2:442-460.
25. "The Scripture Way of Salvation," pp. 447-48.

Notes

Covenant Discipleship
The Early Methodist Class Meeting
for the Church of Today

COVENANT DISCIPLESHIP CONGREGATIONAL KIT
Includes *Discovering the Modern Methodists,* two videocassettes with David Lowes Watson. An 80-minute presentation on a. Muscle in the Church, b. Dynamics of Discipleship, c. Early Methodist Class Meeting, d. Covenant Discipleship Groups. Covenant Discipleship vinyl three-ring binder containing *Covenant Discipleship Congregational Guide, Covenant Discipleship Quarterly* (issues 1-7) and other items. One copy each of *Accountable Discipleship,* the member's handbook; *The Early Methodist Class Meeting,* and 10 brochures to share with interested persons. Order no. M286P. NOT RETURNABLE.

COVENANT DISCIPLESHIP MEMBER'S KIT
Each member of a Covenant Discipleship group needs a *Covenant Discipleship Member's Kit,* which includes *Accountable Discipleship* (the member's handbook), 7 issues of *Covenant Discipleship Quarterly* and other materials in a handsome matching vinyl three-ring binder. Also included is a member's guide, welcoming you to the Covenant Discipleship group and introducing you to its responsibilities. Order no. M287P. NOT RETURNABLE.

ACCOUNTABLE DISCIPLESHIP
Handbook for Covenant Discipleship Groups in the Congregation
This basic resource by David Lowes Watson provides the reader with essential historical and theological foundations of this early Methodist tradition, a step-by-step process by which to form CD groups, and its implications for ministry today. Order no. DR009B.

DISCIPULOS RESPONSABLES
Desarrollar Grupos de Discipulado Cristiano en la Iglesia Local
Accountable Discipleship
En este libro, el autor presenta una excelente base para la formación desarrollo y acción de grupos de discipulos responsables en nuestra Iglesia. Por David L. Watson. Presentado por Mortimer Arias. Order no. F023B.

THE EARLY METHODIST CLASS MEETING
Its Origins and Significance
Written by David Lowes Watson, this basic resource introduces the modern reader to the early Methodist class meeting. Guidelines for using the class meeting in local congregations are also offered. Order no. DR017B.

WESLEY SPEAKS ON CHRISTIAN VOCATION
From a theme of Christian vocation, Paul Wesley Chilcote has assembled selections from the literature by the Wesleys on "What do we teach?", "How do we teach?", and "What do we do?". Wesley speaks clearly to our turbulent times about doctrine, liturgy, worship, hunger, oppression, peace, and service in the world. Reflection questions follow each chapter. Order no. DR041B.

The above titles are available from Discipleship Resources, P.O. Box 189, 1908 Grand Ave., Nashville, TN 37202 (615-340-7284).